IMAGES
*of America*

# HAZLET
# TOWNSHIP

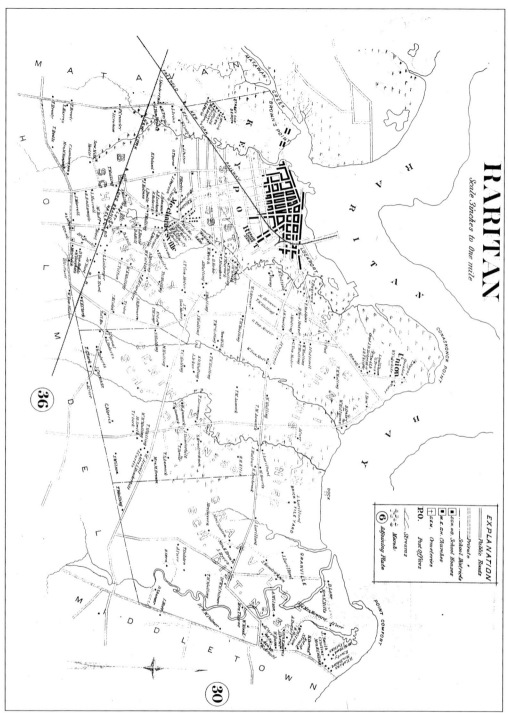

This map shows Raritan (later Hazlet) Township in 1889.

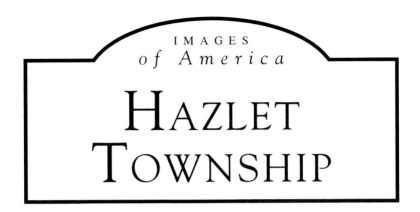

IMAGES
*of America*

# HAZLET
# TOWNSHIP

William B. Longo

ARCADIA
PUBLISHING

Published by Arcadia Publishing
Charleston, South Carolina

Printed in the United States of America

Library of Congress Catalog Card Number: 2008941575

For all general information contact Arcadia Publishing at:
Telephone 843-853-2070
Fax 843-853-0044
E-mail sales@arcadiapublishing.com
For customer service and orders:
Toll-Free 1-888-313-2665

Visit us on the Internet at www.arcadiapublishing.com

*This book is dedicated to the people of Hazlet,
to those still here and to those who are gone.*

*People like my mother, Mary Longo, who raised three children here,
and taught uncounted young residents at the elementary level.*

*People like J. Carlton Cherry, who first invited this, then young, author
to a Hazlet Historical Society meeting. Mr. Cherry served as a mayor
of then Raritan Township and with many others, led and helped to shape
Hazlet's future. Meanwhile, information and photographs preserved over the years
by the Cherry family served as a starting point for this collection.*

*Finally, this book is dedicated to those people who may in the future
choose Hazlet as a place to live.*

# Contents

# Acknowledgments

As with an actor on stage, many behind-the-scenes people are depended upon to assure the show is the best possible. This author is grateful to so many old and new friends who contributed to the final product. The following people gave generously of their time and personal collections: Lillian Cherry, Fred Dean, Tom and Joyce Gallo, Kathi Gannon, Lester Horner (photographer), Bert and Judy Morris.

The following people and organizations loaned photographs from their albums: Marie Artelli, Elmer Bahrenberg, Mrs. Dorothy Bennet, Nancy Cherry, Fred Dean, James Gallo, Tony Kozielski, Hazlet Fire Company No. 1, the Hazlet Police Department, the Hazlet Township Library, Glen Hourihan, Tony Jackapino, Jack and Angel Jeandron, the Keyport Historical Society, the Keyport Public Library, Frank Miele, Jack and Ann Mills, Mr. and Mrs. Frank Mocci, Joe Mocci, Phil Nobile, Catherine Nolan, the North Centerville Fire Company, Frances Palmer, Joel Rosenbaum, Maureen Sweeney, the West Keansburg Fire Company, and Fred Yaeger.

# Introduction

The township of Raritan was created by an act of the New Jersey State Legislature on February 25, 1848, taking 35 square miles away from Middletown Township. In addition to the present Hazlet Township, the township originally included what are now Aberdeen and Holmdel Townships, the boroughs of Keyport, Matawan, and Union Beach, and part of Keansburg Borough. In 1857, Holmdel Township was formed, taking with it 18 square miles. Matawan Township also separated in 1857, taking another 8 square miles away from Raritan Township. (Eventually, Matawan Township was divided into Matawan Borough and Matawan Township, with Matawan Township's name changing to Aberdeen Township in 1977.) Keyport Borough was formed in 1908, and Keansburg Borough was formed in 1917. When Union Beach Borough was formed in 1925, Raritan Township was down to 5.6 square miles.

The name "Raritan" indirectly came from a Native American tribe from Somerset County, where the town of Raritan Borough was formed. There is a major river that runs through Somerset County, which was named the Raritan River. The river flows southeast through New Brunswick and on to Perth Amboy, where it flows into a bay. This bay eventually became the Raritan Bay. So the township of Raritan was actually named after the Raritan Bay as the township, before the breakup, had 5 miles of Raritan Bay shoreline as its northern boundary.

Hazlet came about in 1879, when the Hazlet Post Office was established. Though initially a small section of Raritan Township, the township's name would be changed to Hazlet Township in 1967. The name "Hazlet" came from an individual, Dr. John Hazlett, who had an estate in Raritan Township near the Keyport-Holmdel Turnpike (now Holmdel Road). In 1875, the New York and Long Branch Railroad (now New Jersey Transit's North Jersey Coast Line) was completed, and the railroad line passed near the property of Dr. Hazlett. A railroad station was established on the Keyport-Holmdel Turnpike, mostly to serve farmers so produce could be shipped to cities.

Although the area near the new train station was known as Bethany (as in Bethany Road), the name Bethany was not prominent enough to carry the name of the train station. So the railroad station went by the name of Holmdel, presumably because the depot was on the Keyport-Holmdel Turnpike, which leads to Holmdel. Two years later, the United States Postal Authority decided to open a post office at the train station. But since there was already a Holmdel post office in the village of Holmdel 4 miles to the south, the postal authorities said that another name would have to be used. That is when they chose Hazlett, after the man whose property bordered the north side of the tracks. The railroad then changed the station name to Hazlett, the second "t" was dropped, and "Hazlet" was born.

From 1879 through the mid-1950s, Hazlet, with its railroad station and post office, was a quiet, rural hamlet situated within the township of Raritan. As was true of the former Bethany, the unincorporated community of Hazlet also extended into the northwest portion of Holmdel Township. By 1925, with Raritan Township at its present 5.6 square miles, the township's sections were Mechanicsville (sometimes known as South Keyport), Hazlet, North Centerville, and West Keansburg. The township has remained this size ever since. As it developed, beginning in the 1950s, it lost its rural character and the individual sections became unified into one larger community.

# One

# Rural Beginnings

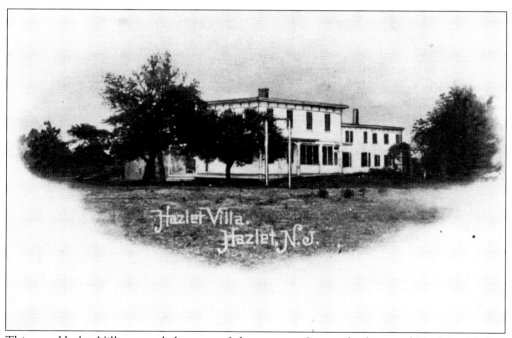

This was Hazlet Villa around the turn of the century. It was the home of Dr. John Hazlett (Hazlett with two t's), from which the township (with one t) derives its name. The house, which is no longer standing, was on the site of the Hazlet Youth Athletic field.

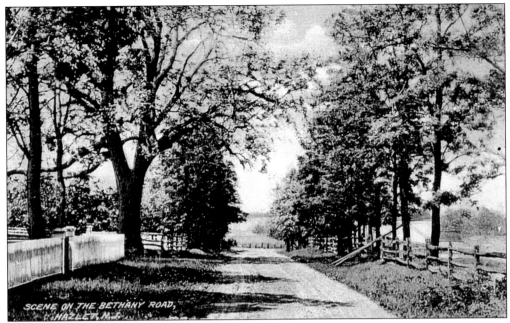

This image was taken of a very rural Bethany Road in 1914. Note the dirt road and open farmland. Bethany (a religious name) was possibly given to the area by early residents before the name Hazlet. Today Bethany Road is a very busy main artery through the area.

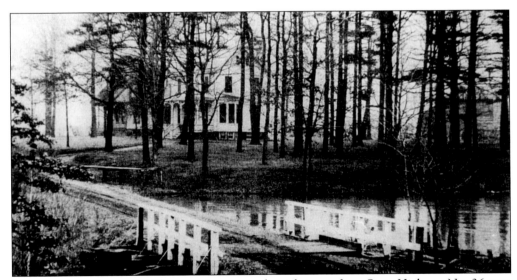

This is a view of a wooded Florence Avenue, a short distance from State Highway No. 36 near the car wash. The bridge foundation also served as a dam, creating Carhart Pond. Today, the pond and the dam are gone.

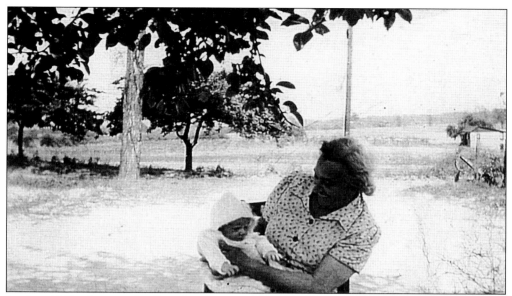

In this 1941 photograph, Grandmother Emma Rudiger holds Bertrum "Bert" Morris. The Rudiger's owned a chicken-raising farm on Hazlet Avenue (seen here), having moved from New Egypt, New Jersey.

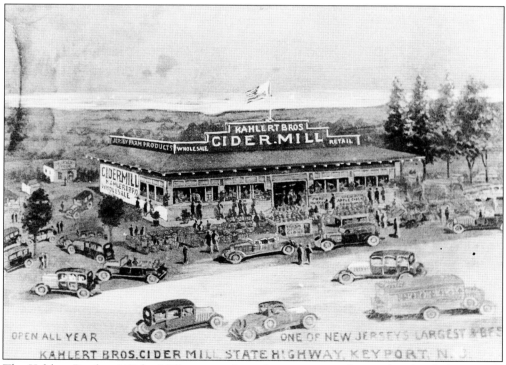

The Kahlert Brothers' Cider Mill, as seen from the air, was on the north side of what is now State Highway No. 35, at the present site of Chelsea Place. In this artist's rendition, there is much activity as customers shop for farm produce and cider.

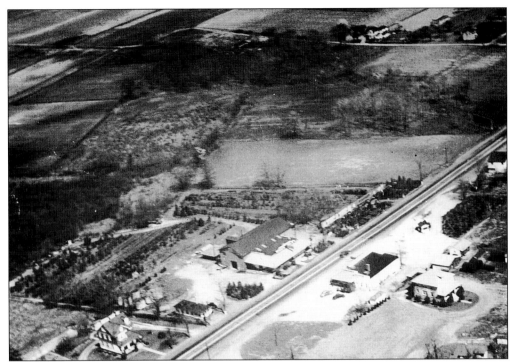

This view was taken of State Highway No. 35 around 1930, looking southeast. It is easy to see how rural the township was at the time. In the foreground is the Hazlet Lunch. On the opposite side of the highway is Ted Kahlert's farm market at the site of Kahlert Brother's Cider Mill (previous photograph). Note the highway was a three-lane roadway, the center lane alternating for north-south traffic.

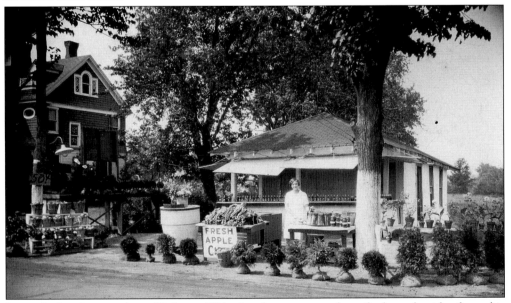

Passersby heading north on Highway 35 had a chance to purchase fresh apple cider from this roadside stand. Open fields are behind the stand. Photograph was taken around 1935. The building on the left was later occupied by a funeral home.

12

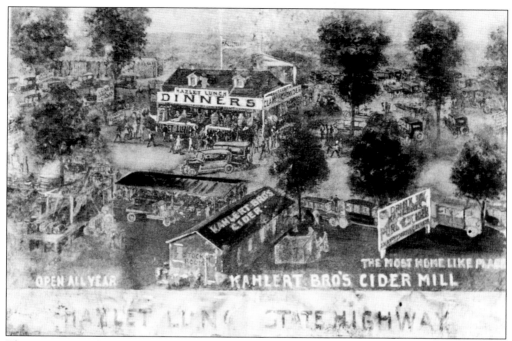

This is a postcard reproduction of the Hazlet Lunch, owned by Bill Kahlert, touched up by an artist. Bill Kahlert was a pilot who owned his own plane. Years later an airplane would be placed on the roof and become a well-known landmark. The Hazlet Lunch closed in the early 1970s and was a disco in 1975.

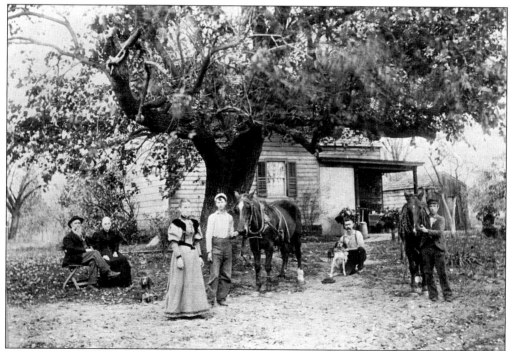

Pictured is the Cook house on Hazlet Avenue. They were a typical farm family, including a dog and a horse, all recording history without realizing it.

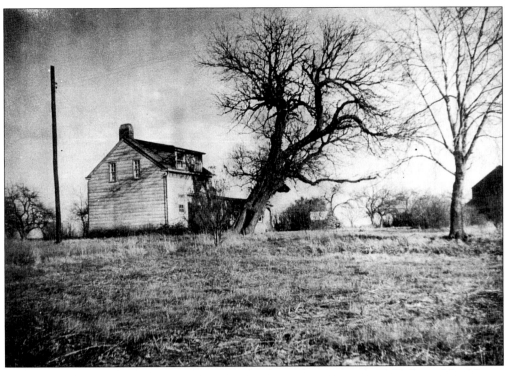

This farmhouse near Hazlet Avenue was most likely on the north side of Highway No. 35.

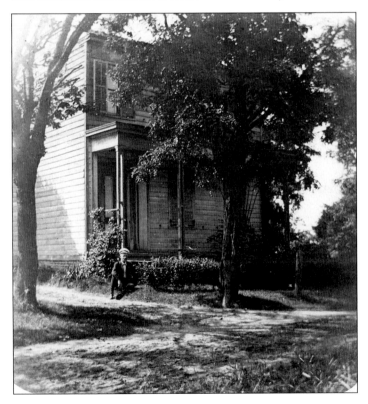

One of the oldest homes in the township is Mr. Harvey's house on Poole Avenue.

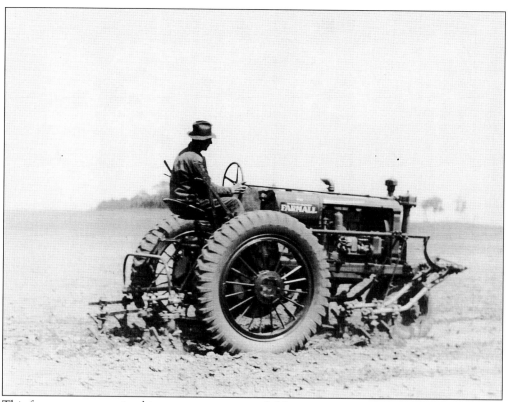

This farmer was operating his tractor on a potato field.

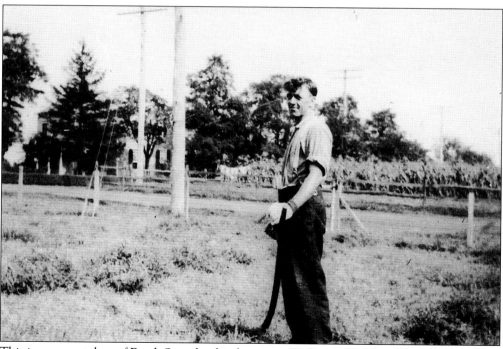

This image was taken of Frank Sprool at his farm near Highway No. 35 and Bethany Road.

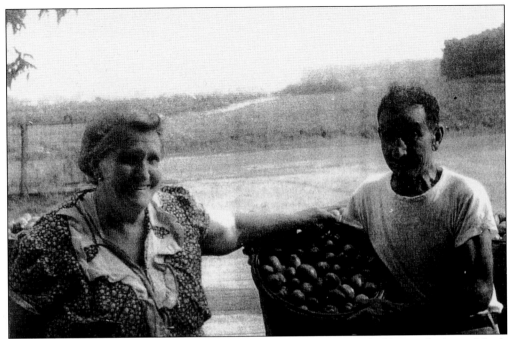

Joe Mocci and his wife, Emilia, are pictured here on their farm holding a basket of fresh vegetables. Joe Mocci emigrated from Italy in 1907 and purchased the Hazlet farm on Bethany Road in 1924. Joe and Emilia raised nine children, with sons Frank, Tobin (Bill), Ralph, and Ernie becoming full partners.

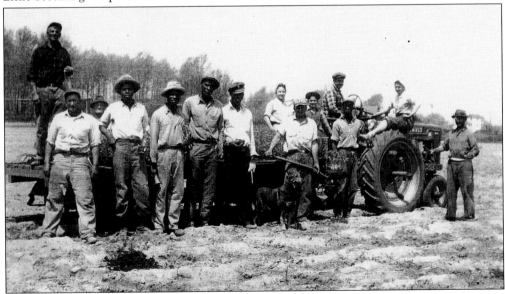

At Joe Mocci's farm, family members and hired hands pose for a photograph in the 1940s. Joe Mocci is on the far right and oldest son Frank is in the driver's seat of the tractor. Bill is standing on the ground to the far left, Ralph is in the center holding a shovel, and the youngest son, Ernie, is sitting between Ralph and Frank. The Mocci daughters also worked hard. Ann is sitting on the trailer and is just to the left of Ralph, while Rose is sitting on the giant tractor wheel, hoping Frank does not put the tractor in gear.

Joe Mocci poses for a picture on his Bethany Road farm, just as he is about to drive a truckload of produce to market. The International Truck was purchased from the Raritan Garage in the Mechanicsville section of the township. Produce from the Mocci farm was taken in trucks to farm markets and produce distribution centers in Newark, Perth Amboy, and New York City. In earlier days, produce was shipped by steamboat (from Keyport) and by train (from Hazlet).

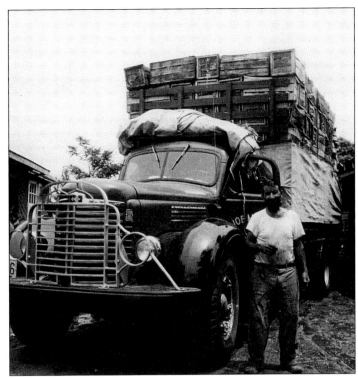

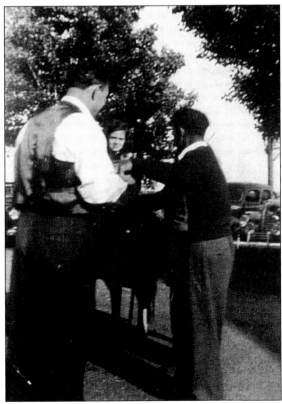

It's recreation time on the Mocci farm as Joe Mocci (far right) helps his granddaughter ride a pony.

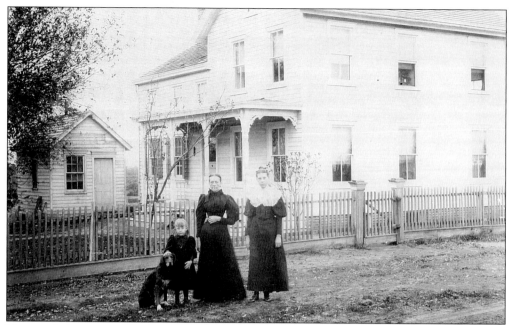

The rural character of Hazlet near the turn of the century is evident in this scene on Hazlet Avenue. Pictured in front of their home are Violet Walling, Josephine Anderson Walling (wife of Wilson Walling), and Dora Walling (later Dora Cherry). This is the site of today's Pep Boys store. Note the small building on the left, which is also shown in the photograph below.

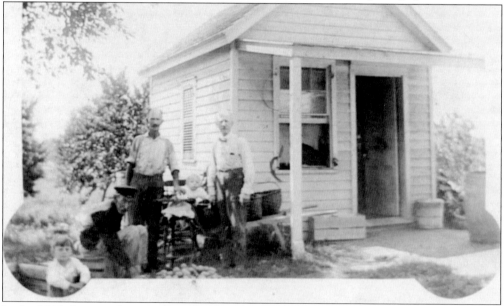

In this 1910 photograph, several people of various ages pose for a picture on the Walling property. The gentleman sitting on the vegetable crate and wearing a hat is Wilson Walling. Standing next to him is Joseph Conover Cherry (left) and Mr. Harvey. In between Mr. Cherry and Mr. Harvey is an infant, J. Carlton Cherry, a future mayor of Raritan (Hazlet) Township. The baby is the grandson of Wilson Walling and the son of Joseph Conover Cherry. The identity of the small boy sitting in the lower left of the photograph is unknown.

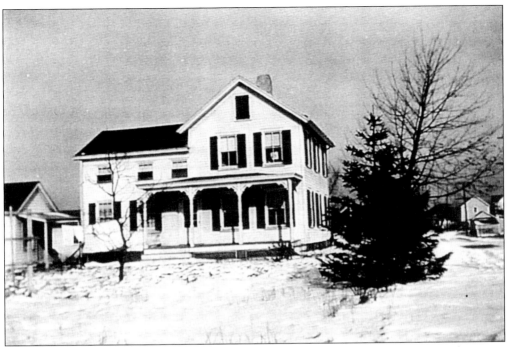

Thirty-six years later, in 1946, J. Carlton Cherry lived with his wife, Lillian, in this house on Hazlet Avenue. This location would become the site of Pep Boys. In the lower photograph, the Cherry's 1940 Chrysler is parked in their driveway.

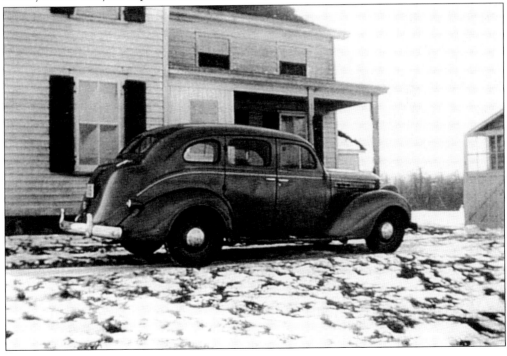

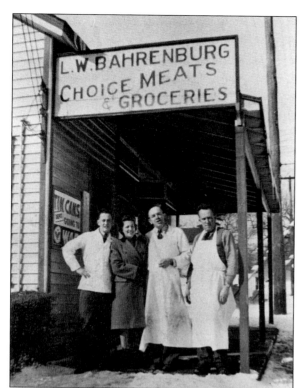

Members of the Bahrenburg family stand in front of their Meats and Groceries Store on Keyport-Holmdel Turnpike. The family also operated a farm on Beers Street.

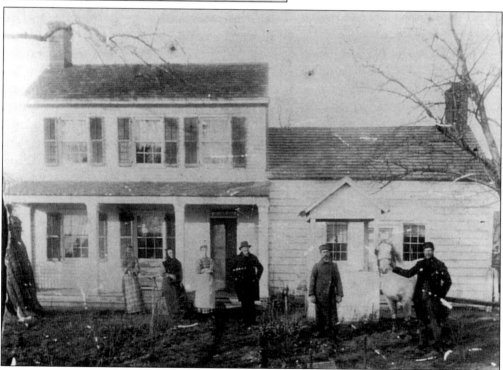

In this image, members of a family pose in front of a homestead on Hazlet Avenue. Note the well, which provided the home's water, including drinking water.

Dominick and Angeline Davino are pictured here on their farm on Florence Avenue. In 1920 they inherited a farmhouse from Giovanni and Josephine Davino. Bradlee's department store would be built across the street much later.

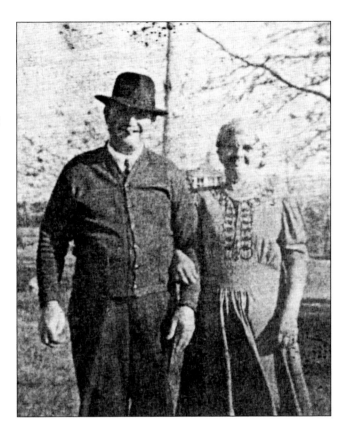

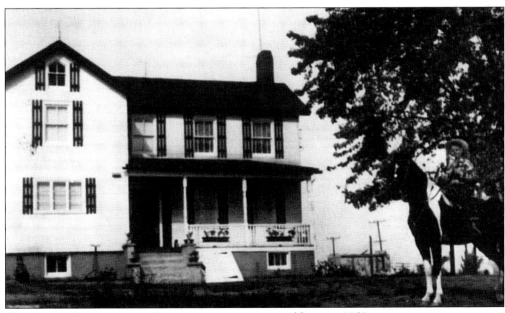

The Davino farmhouse on Florence Avenue is pictured here in 1953.

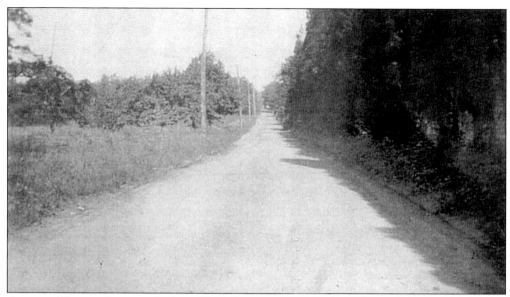

As a neighbor to the more built-up Keansburg, West Keansburg was somewhat rural, as this 1920 view of Laurel Avenue attests.

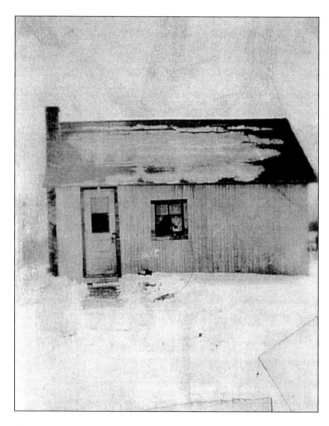

This house was photographed on Essex Street in West Keansburg after a snowstorm.

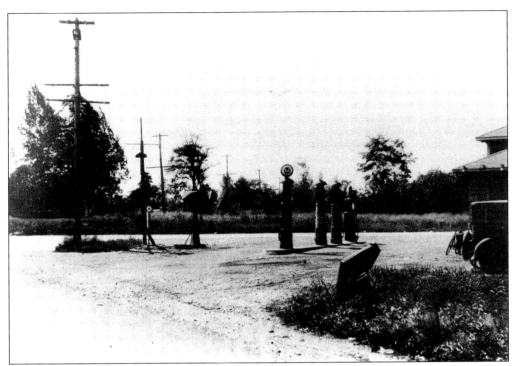

The intersection of Laurel Avenue and State Highway No. 36 in West Keansburg, shown here around 1930, seems uninhabited but still required a gas station; probably serving motorists on their way to Keansburg and other shore points. West Keansburg was generally less rural than the Hazlet and North Centerville sections of the township.

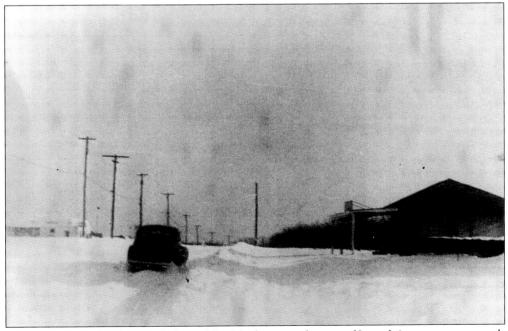

On a snowy stretch of State Highway No. 36, about a mile west of Laurel Avenue, a car travels on the boundary of Hazlet and Union Beach.

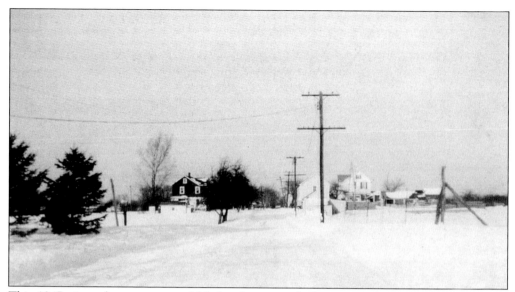

This 1947 view of a snow-covered Hazlet Avenue is looking toward State Highway No. 35. Both houses were owned by Henry and Anna Warnock, whose apple and peach orchards covered several acres along the highway. Asparagus grew closer to the house on the right, with corn, tomatoes, peppers, etc. further up Hazlet Avenue. Foxwood homes now cover this area up to the railroad tracks.

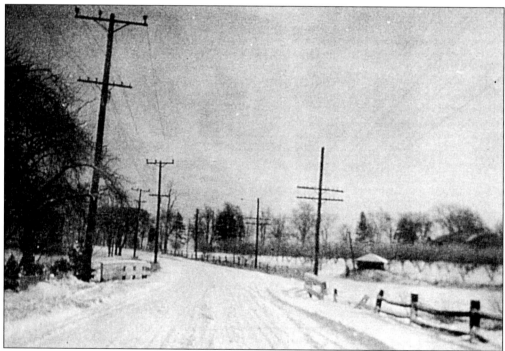

This is a picture of Bethany Road under a foot of snow, just west of Hazlet Pharmacy, looking toward Telegraph Hill Road. Dormant apple trees are visible in the field on the right. Marc Woods homes are now ahead on the left.

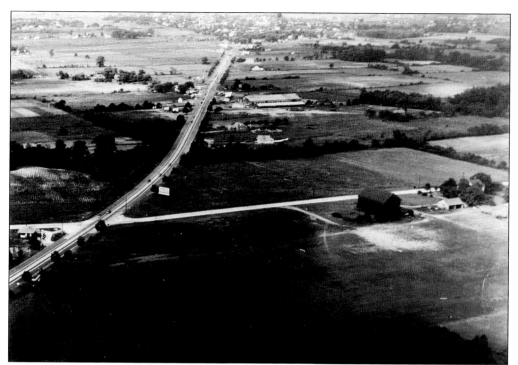

Here is an aerial view of Highway 36 at the intersection of Middle Road in 1948. Today the Airport Plaza Shopping Center is to the right of the highway, and the Academy Bus Station is on the left. In the distance is the Keyport Auction, at the corner of the highway and Poole Avenue. The auction closed around 1963.

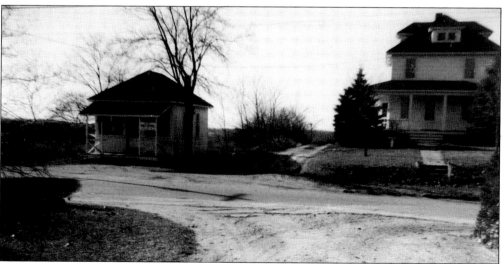

Pictured above is the Hazlet Post Office and postmaster's house on Holmdel Road, around 1949. The small post office provided post office boxes as no deliveries were yet made. Rural deliveries were provided in the area by the Keyport Post Office through the late 1950s. Home deliveries were provided by Hazlet beginning around 1959. The current Hazlet Post Office opened in 1961.

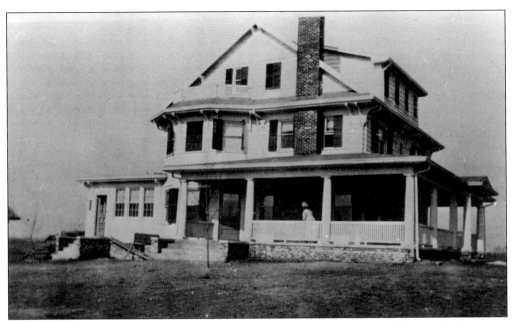

The former Conover farmhouse on Beers Street is still standing located near the Giuseppe Pizzeria and Italian Restaurant.

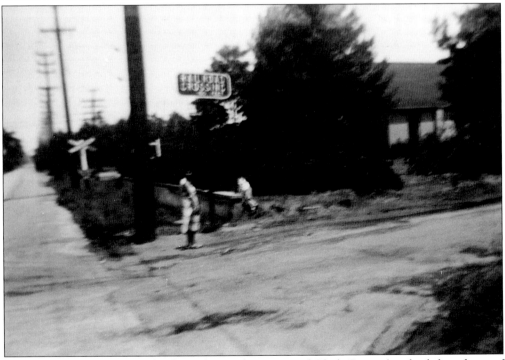

This view was taken from Lloyd Road near the corner of Clark Street (to the left and out of view is today's Aberdeen Township Little League Baseball Field). The railroad crossing is on the Atlantic Highlands branch of the Central Railroad of New Jersey, which also passes through West Keansburg. At this view today is one entrance to the Henry Hudson Trail, a modern use for a defunct rail line.

# *Two*

# Transportation and Roads

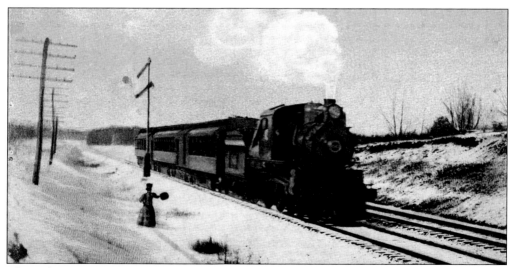

The Atlantic City Express train is seen here speeding southbound through Hazlet at the turn of the century. The location is between Beers Street and Holmdel Road. The woman in the foreground waves her hand muff to those on board the train.

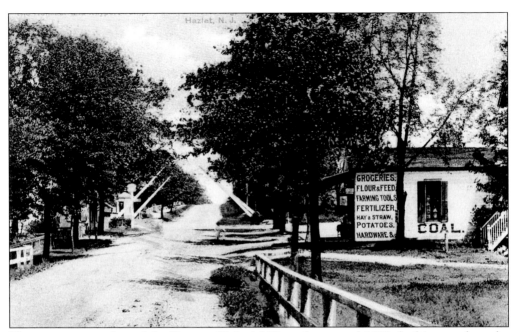

This picture was taken of the Keyport-Holmdel Turnpike around 1900, looking north at the crossing of the New York and Long Branch Railroad. The railroad, which was jointly operated by the Central Railroad of New Jersey and the Pennsylvania Railroad, was completed in 1875. Manually operated crossing gates protect wagon traffic from the busy, two-track railroad line. In 1929, the store on the right would become the home of Swartzel's Hardware and Garden Supplies Store.

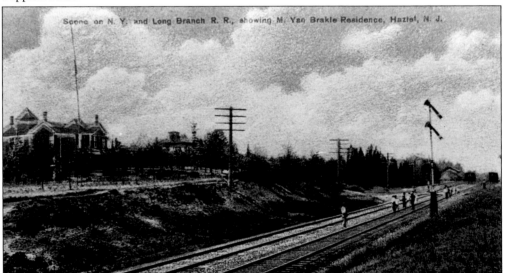

This is an image of the New York and Long Branch Railroad tracks, facing west, between Bethany Road and Hazlet Avenue, which is just ahead. The men appear to be track repairmen. To the far right side of the photograph is the Hazlet Freight Station with several boxcars on sidings. The estate above to the left portion of the photograph is the M. Van Brakle residence. The large house to the right of it is the Brailley Estate (now the Hazlet Train Stop and the residence of Boyd Mason).

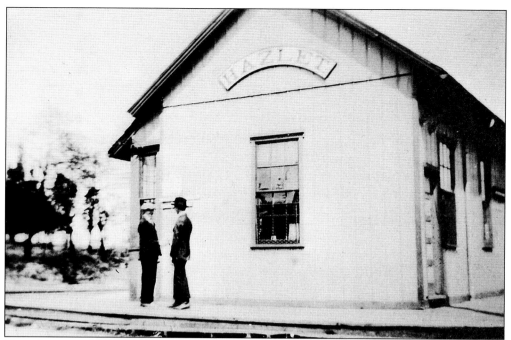

Note the curved bentwood sign on the side of Hazlet's passenger depot. Hazlet was served by Central Railroad of New Jersey trains, which ran to Jersey City. Pennsylvania Railroad trains, which ran directly to New York, did not stop at Hazlet. As residents switched to automobiles, or drove to Matawan (which had better train service), fewer trains served Hazlet. By 1952, when the agency was closed and the station demolished, only three trains were stopping here. Today, Hazlet has excellent train service operated by New Jersey Transit.

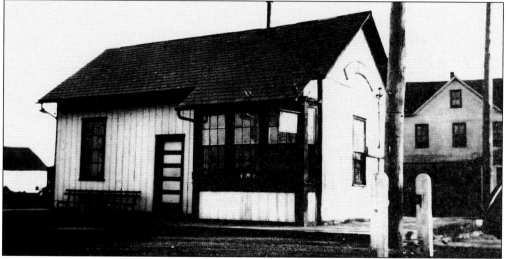

This c. 1939 image of the front view of the passenger station shows Swartzel's Hardware and Farm Supply Store in the background. The freight station, out of view to the left, actually got more usage than the passenger station. Farmers shipped tons of produce from there, at one point up to one hundred boxcars a day. Up to the early 1950s, loads of Christmas trees were delivered to the railroad sidings every November. Use of the freight station and sidings also declined as farmers and other shippers switched to trucks.

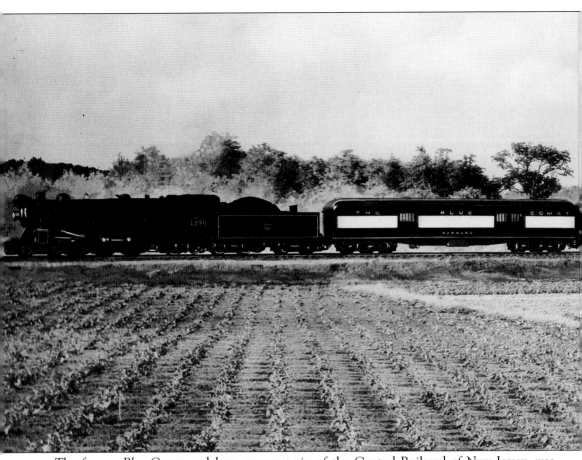

The famous *Blue Comet*, a deluxe express train of the Central Railroad of New Jersey, was captured for a publicity shot behind what is now the K-Mart Shopping Center. The locomotive of the blue-and-cream colored train is facing Bethany Road. The field in the foreground is now Sterling Meadows. The *Blue Comet*, which ran daily from Jersey City to Atlantic City,

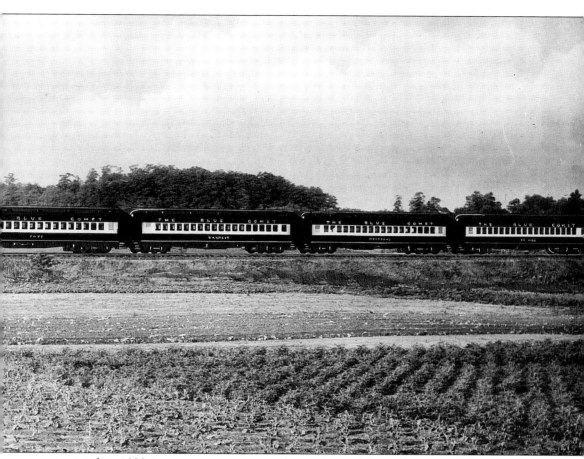

was initiated in 1929 in an attempt to gain a larger share of the still lucrative New York to Atlantic City market from the Pennsylvania Railroad, which operated over a different route. A huge success at first, the *Blue Comet*'s popularity dropped off in the 1930s, and the train was discontinued in 1941 as part of the war conservation efforts.

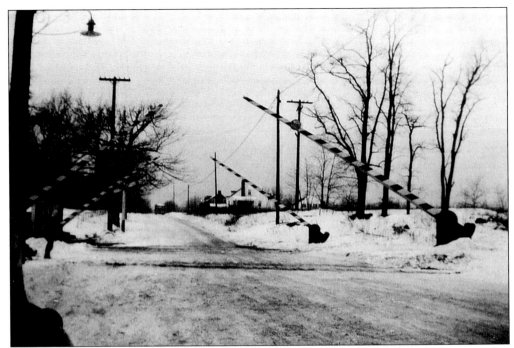

Here is a later view of the railroad crossing at Keyport-Holmdel Turnpike around 1945. By this time, the road was referred to as it is today—Holmdel Road. The crossing protection is still the manual type, but that would be replaced by electric automatic gates with flashing lights in 1953.

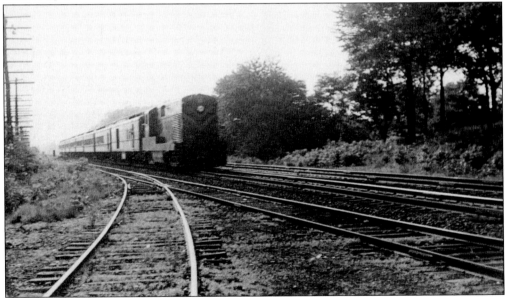

This 1954 shot of a passenger train near Holmdel Road shows two sidings used for shipping freight to local businesses. The track curving to the left went directly to Swartzel's. The Swartzel's siding was torn up in 1968 in order to expand the commuter parking lot. By then, Swartzel's was receiving most large shipments by truck, though they received a few shipments by rail on the other siding in 1969. Mostly unused since then, the other siding was torn up in 1973.

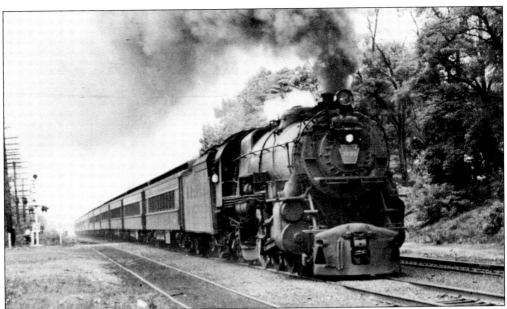

This Pennsylvania Railroad passenger train is running from Pennsylvania Station, New York City, to Bay Head, New Jersey. Pulled by a K-4 type, steam locomotive it speeds through Hazlet in 1955, in this Homer Hill photograph. Note the flashing lights and automatic electric gates at the Holmdel Road crossing.

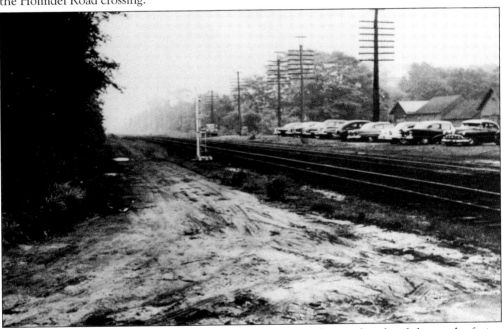

This is another image that was taken of the railroad on the north side of the tracks facing Hazlet Avenue. To the right of the tracks automobiles of commuters are parked for the day. The buildings on the far right are the Swartzel's buildings, which were served by the railroad spur. The tall gadget near the center of the photograph (to the left of the tracks) is an apparatus that allowed a moving train to catch a U.S. Mail bag containing mail from the Hazlet Post Office, which at the time was located on Holmdel Road.

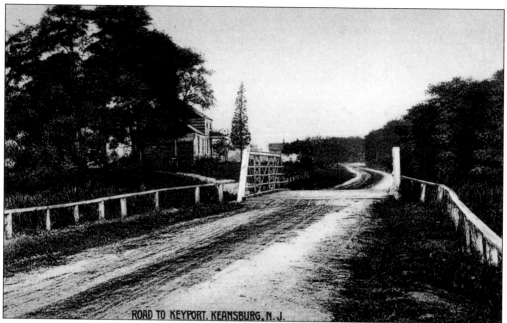

This is a very early 1900s view of what would become State Highway No. 36 in West Keansburg. The bridge spans Waackaack Creek, just west of Palmer Avenue. The future highway had more curves than it has today, as we can see the dirt road winding westward toward Keyport.

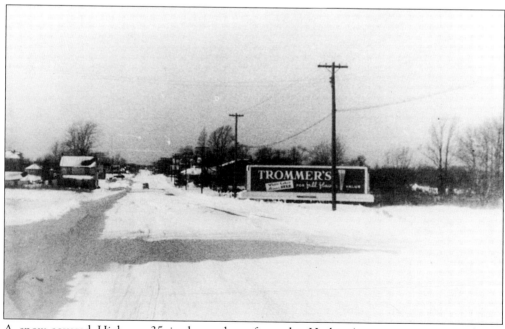

A snow-covered Highway 35 is shown here from the Hazlet Avenue intersection, facing Keyport. Friendly Restaurant is now on the site of the billboard in this picture.

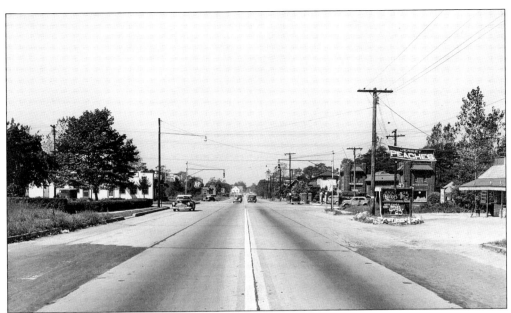

A more recent view of Highway 36 near West Keansburg was captured near the intersection of Palmer Avenue, facing west. This mid-1950s image shows when the highway consisted of one lane for each direction. The highway was expanded to two lanes for each direction, with a concrete divider in the middle, in 1965. The banner on the right markets "Jersey Peaches" while a lower sign offers "Jersey Potatoes."

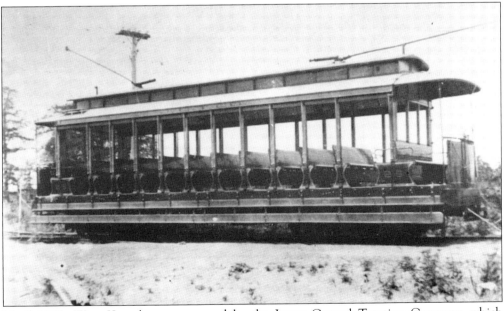

Until 1923, West Keansburg was served by the Jersey Central Traction Company, which operated trolleys between Keyport and Campbell's Junction in Middletown Township. The trolley tracks passed through West Keansburg between Eighth Street and Ninth Street, where today there is an open median between the two streets. Here is a view of one of the trolley cars that passed daily through the township.

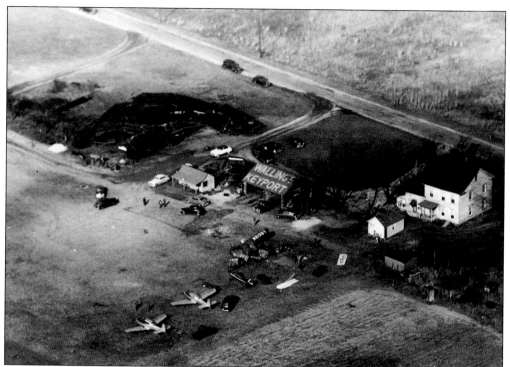

Nobody ever thinks of leaving or arriving Hazlet by air, but until 1958 the township had an airport! The Walling Field was located near the corner of Highway 36 and Middle Road. Until the early 1960s, this part of the township was considered an extension of Keyport, hence that name on the roof of the hanger. In 1959 the airport was relocated to Morganville (Marlboro Township), and a shopping center opened at this site. The shopping center is (you guessed it) the Airport Plaza Shopping Center.

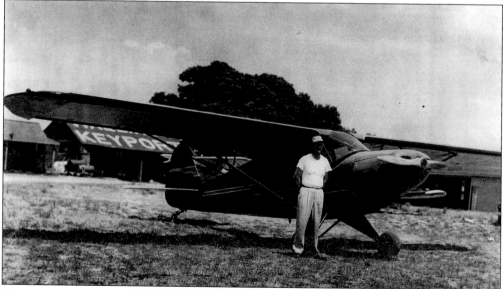

Pilot Richard Cressman stands in front of his plane in 1958, just before the airport was moved from the township.

# *Three*

# Business

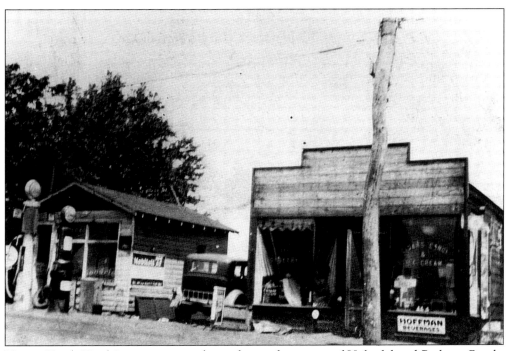

Here is Frank Hertle's grocery store, located near the corner of Holmdel and Bethany Roads. This is only a few hundred feet from Dean's Atlantic Gasoline Station on Bethany Road. The Deans and Hertles were related. The grocery store was so close to Bethany Road that it was often struck by automobiles as a result of collisions at the intersection.

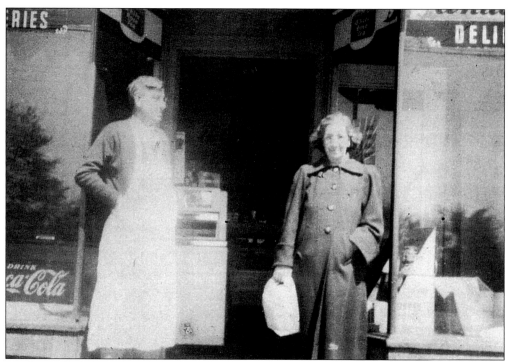

Frank Hertle and his sister, Anna Hertle Dean, are standing here in front of their store where many residents from both Hazlet and Holmdel did their shopping.

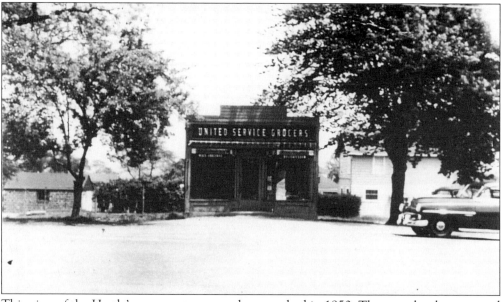

This view of the Hertle's grocery store was photographed in 1950. The store has been moved away from Bethany Road, and the gas station has been relocated to the corner of Holmdel and Bethany Roads. Ten years later, the grocery store would move to a new building on the other side of Holmdel Road, which allowed for the expansion of the Esso gas station. The old grocery store building would be moved 100 feet north to be used as a barbershop. It is now Gentlemen's Choice.

Standing in front of J.H. Bahrenburg's Meat Market is Mr. Bahrenburg. This business also served residents of Hazlet and Holmdel. The building today is the home of the Hazlet Deli and Greek Store, across from the railroad station.

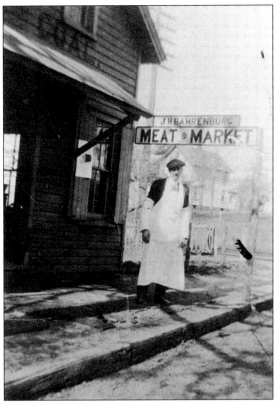

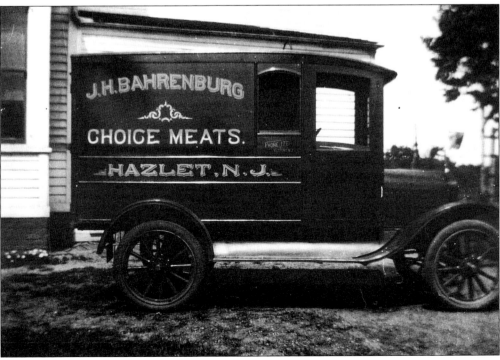

Here is Mr. Bahrenburg's truck advertising the business.

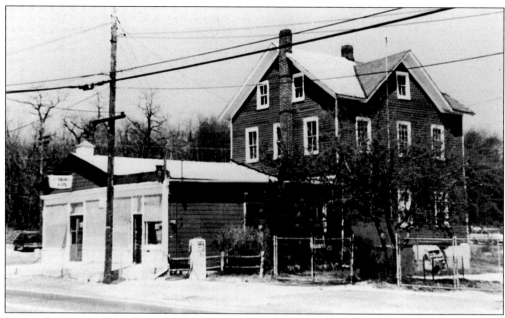

Swartzel's Farm and Garden Supplies is pictured here as it appeared in 1960. Prior to Swartzel's business being established in 1926, the main building shown here was a tavern/hotel and later a general store. In the 19th century a stagecoach line operated between Keyport, Holmdel Village, Colts Neck, and Freehold with the hotel/tavern serving as a designated stop along the busy route.

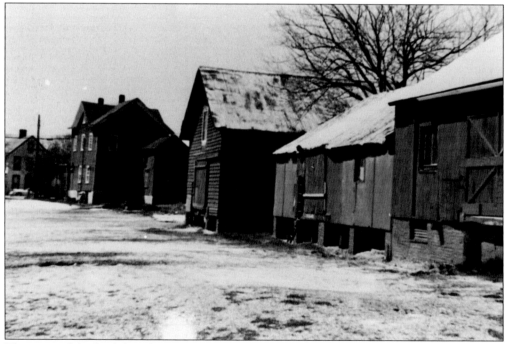

This view of the back-lot of Swartzel's shows buildings that stored items such as fertilizers, pet foods, feeds, seeds, and galvanized materials. Through the 1960s the store served farmers not only from Hazlet, but also from nearby Holmdel, Middletown, Marlboro, and Colts Neck.

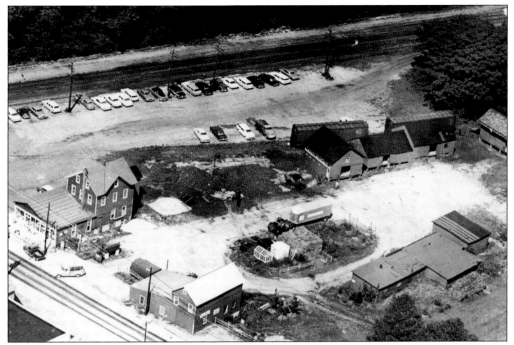

This aerial view shows the Swartzel's Farm and Garden Supplies Center. The parking lot in the upper portion of the photograph is the Hazlet Railroad Station commuter parking lot. Notice the two boxcars likely containing goods to be sold by Swartzel's. (Photograph courtesy of *The Courier*.)

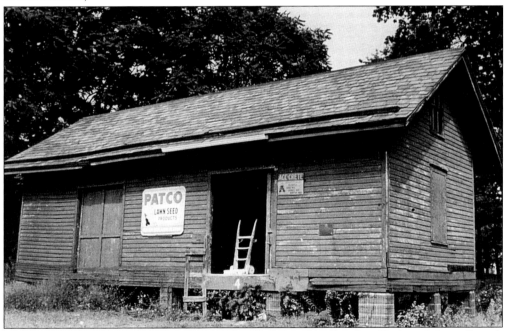

This building was the former Hazlet Freight Station. After the New York and Long Branch Railroad closed the freight station, Swartzel's purchased the building, moving it to their own property for storage use.

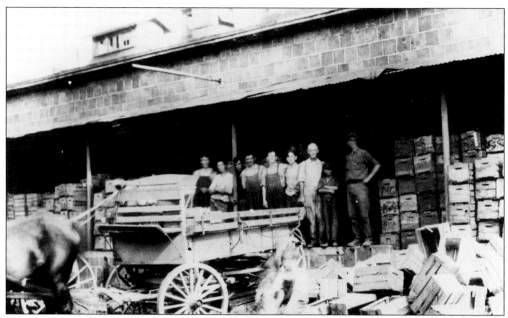

Located north of the railroad tracks near Hazlet Avenue is the Vecchi Catchup Factory. Locally grown tomatoes were used, as were apples for the autumn production of cider and apple butter. After World War II the factory was used for making metal products, but closed around 1960. It was demolished in 1963. However, the tall chimney stands today, as a monument from an earlier time marking the unofficial crossroads of the township's early commerce, the railroad and Keyport-Holmdel Turnpike, so close to the site of Dr. John Hazlett's villa.

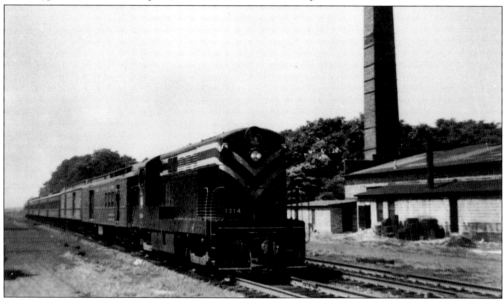

This view of the Vecchi factory building with a passenger train passing by was taken around 1954. This is now the site of the railroad station commuter parking lot near Hazlet Avenue, marked by the tall chimney. Note that there are several mail-carrying cars on this train. However, like the factory, by the mid-1960s they would be gone as mail contracts were won by airlines and trucks.

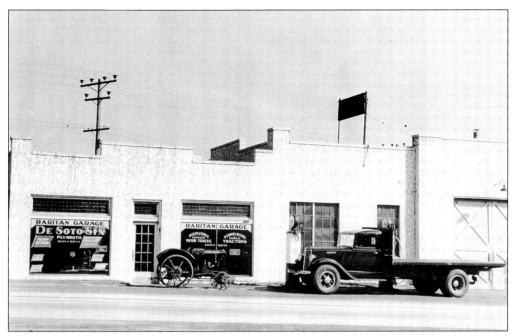

The Raritan Garage is pictured here, on the corner of South Main Street, Bedle Road, and Highway No. 35. Here you could buy trucks and tractors, something needed by farmers in the area.

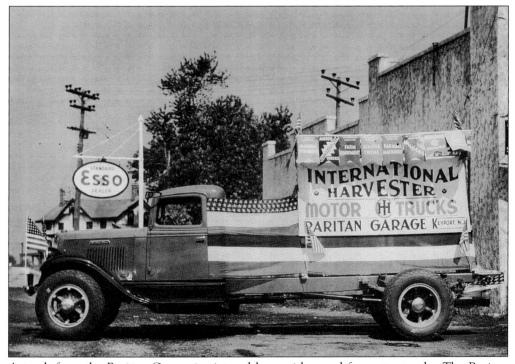

A truck from the Raritan Garage is pictured here with an ad for motor trucks. The Raritan Garage often used Keyport, New Jersey, as its address, although it was actually in Raritan (Hazlet) Township, of which Keyport had once been a part.

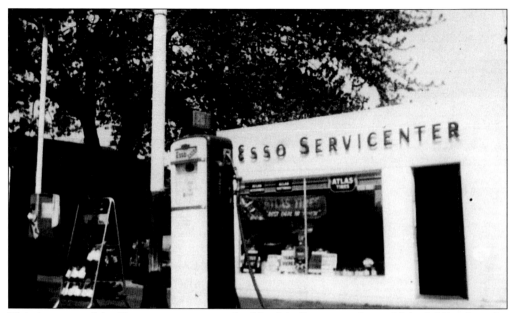

This image is of the Esso station next to the Hertle's Groceries, facing Holmdel Road at the corner of Bethany Road. Today this is the Philly Lube.

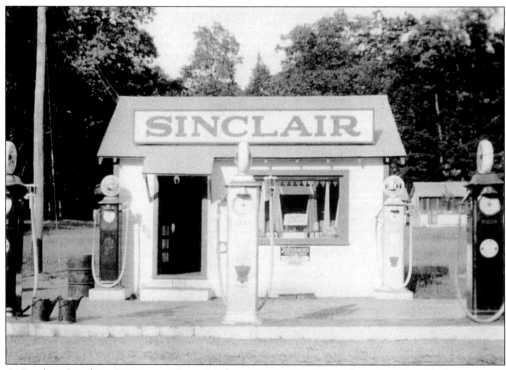

A Sinclair Gasoline Station, on State Highway 36 in West Keansburg, is pictured above.

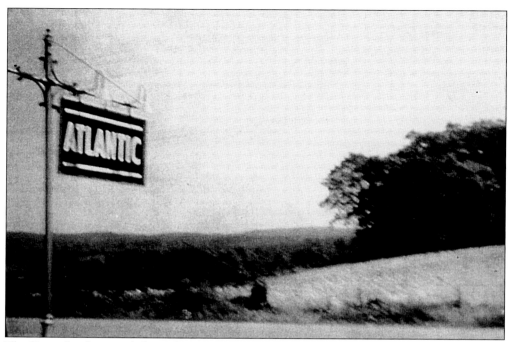

The Dean family owned the Atlantic Gas Station on Bethany Road. Here is an image of the Atlantic sign, facing Bethany Road looking toward Holmdel.

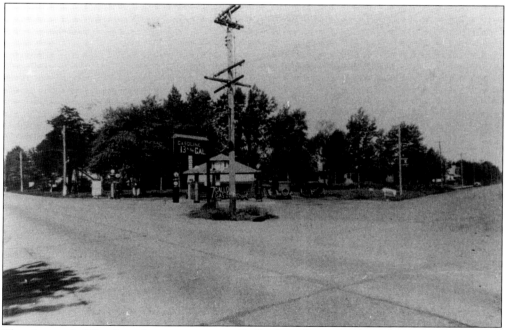

The sign reads "Gasoline thirteen cents per Gallon" in this 1931 photograph. The gas station is at the corner of Highway 36 and Laurel Avenue in West Keansburg. The price of gas may sound like a bargain, but considering the country had been hit by the Great Depression, many motorists most likely could not afford to "fill 'er up."

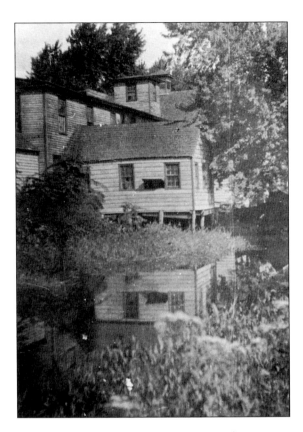

This mill is near the boundary of Keyport in the Mechanicsville section of the township.

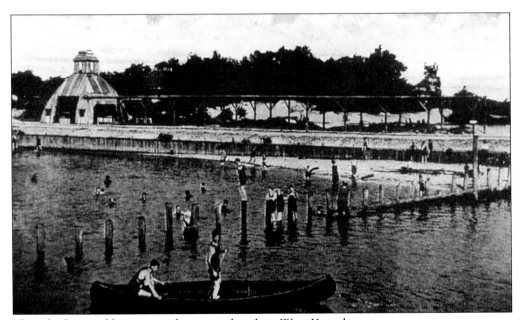

These bathers and boaters are shown at a beach in West Keansburg.

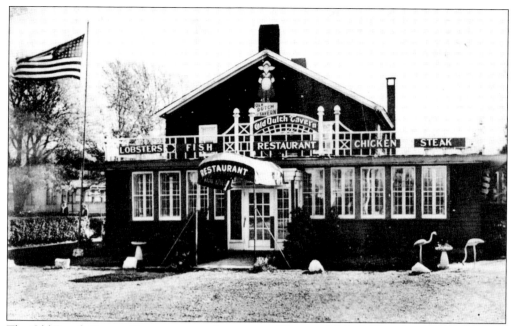

The Old Dutch Tavern Restaurant, on the corner of Keyport-Holmdel Road and State Highway No. 35, was owned and operated by the Mariolis family. The restaurant became the Shore Point Inn, a long-standing icon of Hazlet for both tourists heading for the Jersey Shore and us locals. After a fire in 1965, it was rebuilt remaining the Shore Point Inn. Thirty years later the name became the Cove II; currently, it is the Sea Gull, serving old and new generations.

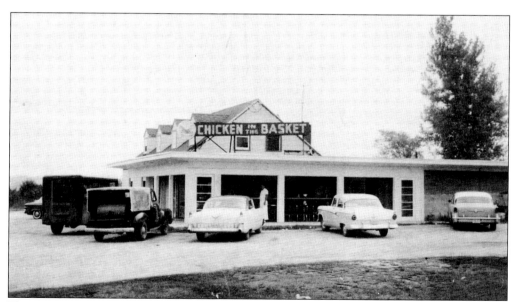

This view is from the 1950s. The restaurant is the "Chicken in the Basket" near Natco Lake on the Hazlet side of State Highway No. 36. Owner O.F. Orton can be seen standing in the doorway. Today, this is the sight of the Lakeside Manor Restaurant.

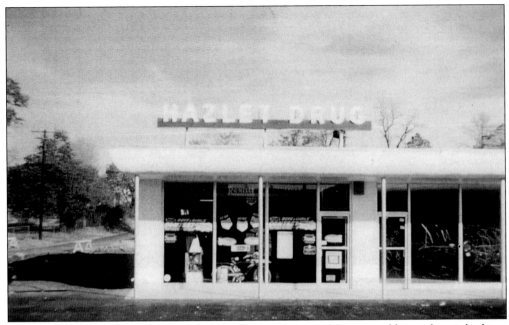

The Hazlet Drug Store (officially called the Hazlet Pharmacy) is pictured here when it had just opened in 1959. This is at the corner of Bethany Road and Hazlet Avenue. About 15 years later the pharmacy was enlarged, and is still in operation today.

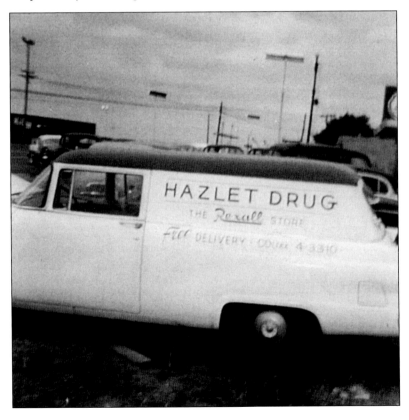

The Hazlet Drug Store made deliveries. Here is a photograph of their delivery station wagon.

# *Four*

# Serving the Township

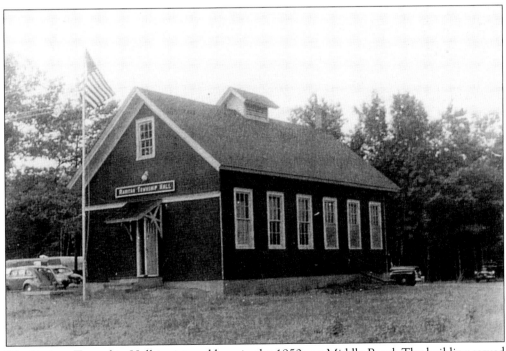

The Raritan Township Hall is pictured here in the 1950s on Middle Road. The building served as the North Centerville School until 1952, at which time the township's board of education gave the building to the township. By the late 1960s, the township administration's needs outgrew the small building. This building became the library.

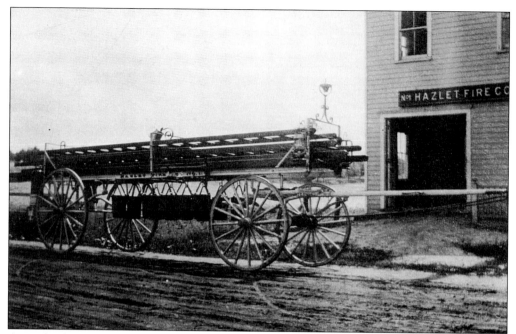

An early photograph was taken here of the Hazlet Fire Company building on Keyport-Holmdel Road. The Hazlet Fire Company was organized in 1910. It was formed as a result of a fire in 1909 that destroyed the local railroad freight station.

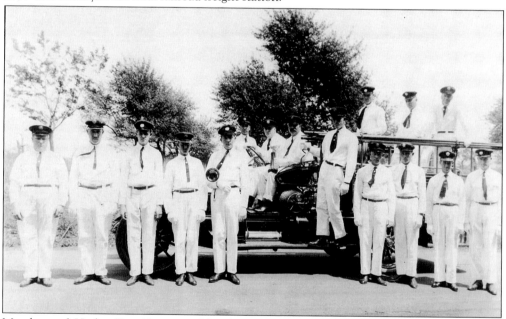

Members of Hazlet Fire Company No. 1 are posing at the Monmouth County Fair in Middletown around 1916 with their Simplex Fire Engine. From left to right they are as follows: (on the ground) Frank Hyer, Howard Guillaudeau, Harry Peseux, Edward Hanaway, Clarence Bahrenburg, Roy Lambertson, Morris Longstreet, Harry Cowles, and Joseph Peseux; (on the truck) Howard Walling, Peter O. Weigand Jr., Charles Crawford, Sidney Pedee, Clarance Pedee, Alonzo Layton, and Hiram Duryea.

Roy Clark is at the wheel of the Hazlet Fire Department's first motorized truck about 1922. The truck was made from a converted simplex touring car.

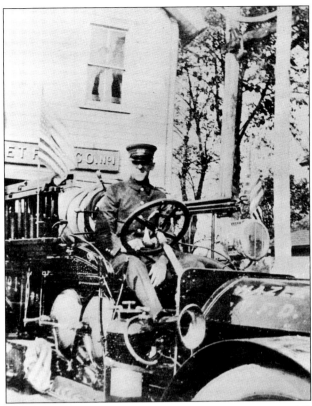

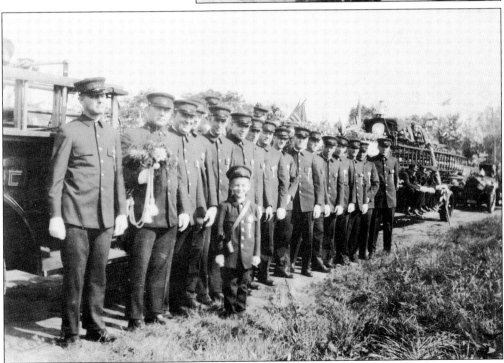

Members of the Hazlet Fire Company No. 1 get ready for a parade in Keyport in 1928.

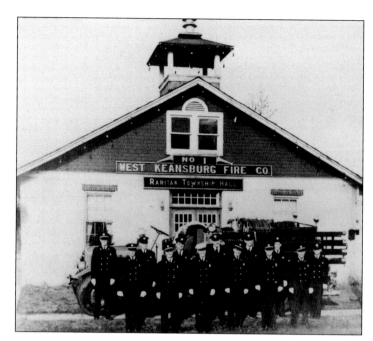

The West Keansburg Fire Company is pictured here on Eighth Street in 1927. Note that the township did not always have a separate township hall building, and for many years the township affairs and meetings were held in various homes. But by 1927, the West Keansburg Firehouse also served as the township hall. At that time, West Keansburg was more developed than the Hazlet and North Centerville sections, so it made sense to establish the township hall there.

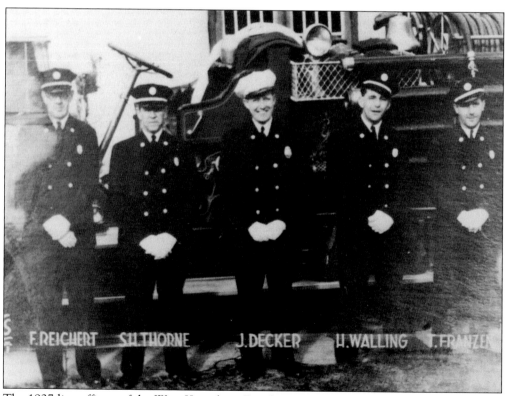

F. REICHERT    S.L. THORNE    J. DECKER    H. WALLING    T. FRANZEN

The 1927 line officers of the West Keansburg Fire Company pose for a photograph.

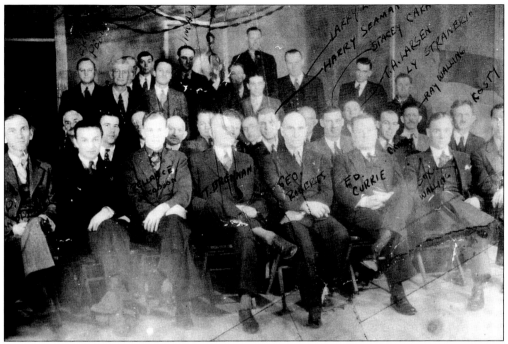

A group of township officials met at the North Centerville Firehouse. Among those present are Ernest Peseux, Jim Aumack, Larry Larsen, Harry Seaman, Stacey Carhart, T.A. Larsen, Ly Straniero, Ray Walling, "Sox" Walling, Ed Currie, George Roberts, Tom Brennan, Reliance Jacobsen, Ed Vanderbilt, and J. Carlton Cherry.

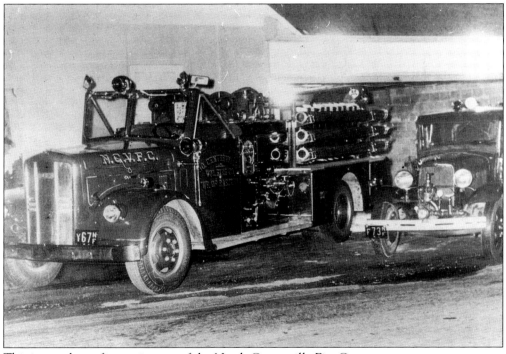

This image shows fire equipment of the North Centerville Fire Company.

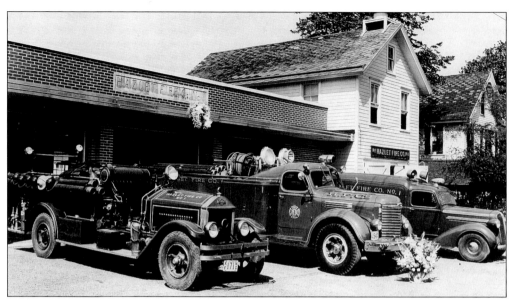

In this view of the Hazlet Fire Company building in 1946, a lot has changed from earlier images. The building is considerably larger. The construction of a new three-bay wing, connected to the original two-story building, had recently been completed. This addition was made possible by a large donation from Joe Mocci, of the Joe Mocci and Sons Farm. All four of Joe's sons—Frank, Bill, Ralph, and Ernie—became members of the Hazlet Fire Company.

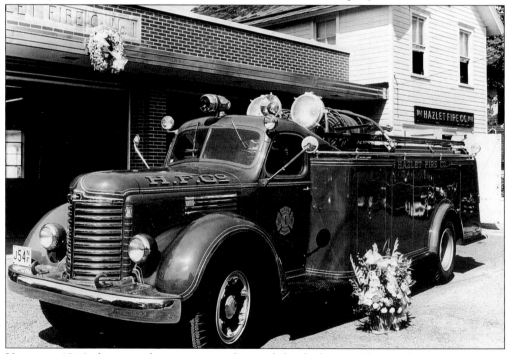

Here is a 1946 close-up of an engine in front of the firehouse. The Hazlet Fire Company eventually found a new home a quarter of a mile north of here, in 1975, where they are located today. In the 1980s, the former firehouse was remodeled into offices visible as 648 Holmdel Road.

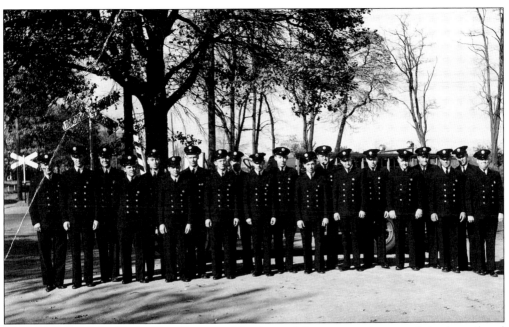

The members of the Hazlet Fire Company No. 1 posed for a group photograph in the railroad station parking lot in 1948. The street on the left is Holmdel Road.

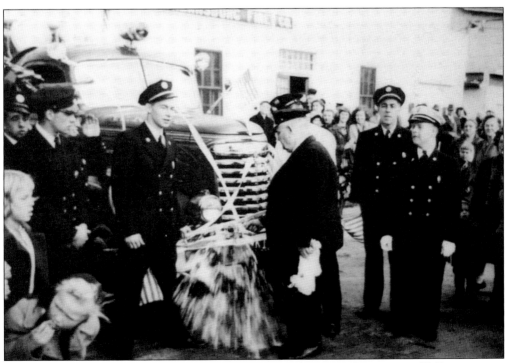

A wet-down was captured on camera at the West Keansburg Fire Company in 1949.

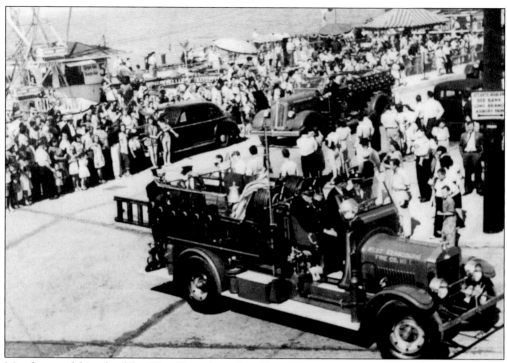

Members and friends of the West Keansburg Fire Company participate in a parade in Keansburg, seen turning the corner of Beachway and Carr Avenues, in the late 1940s.

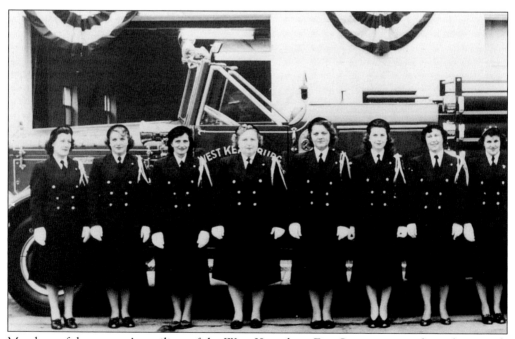

Members of the women's auxiliary of the West Keansburg Fire Company pose for a photograph during a wet-down on October 27, 1956.

Members of the
West Keansburg
Fire Company
meet outside
the firehouse on
Eighth Street in
the 1950s.

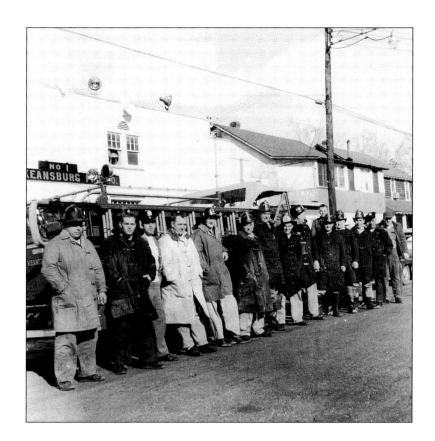

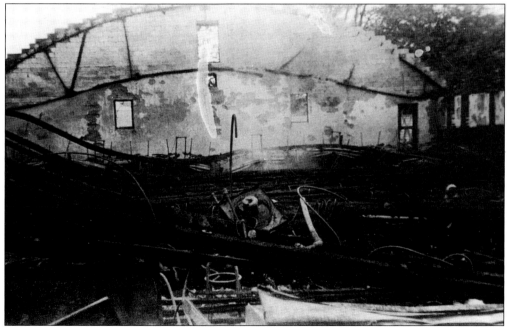

This burned-out bowling alley was located on Highway No. 35, around 1946, near today's
Remson's Dodge. Fire companies from Hazlet as well as neighboring towns fought this blaze.

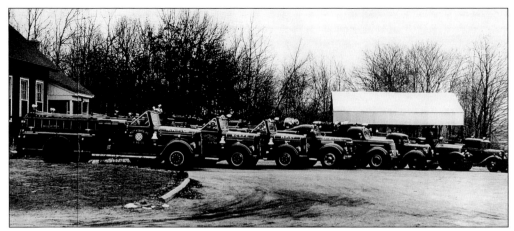

The firetrucks from all three township fire companies are rounded up for a group shot in the 1950s at the township hall on Middle Road. The area still had a rural look to it.

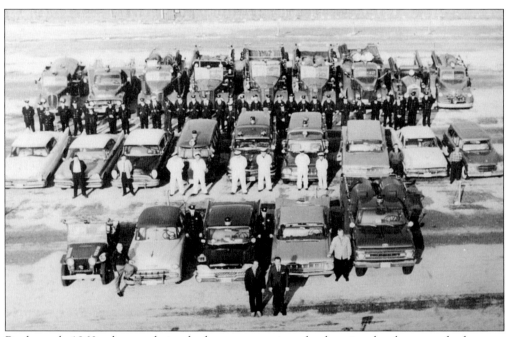

By the early 1960s, the population had grown, as quite a few housing developments had sprung up throughout the township. In this 1960 photograph, it is apparent that the number of trucks of the township's three fire companies has also grown. Here the trucks and many members are on view at Loew's Drive-In Theater on Highway 35.

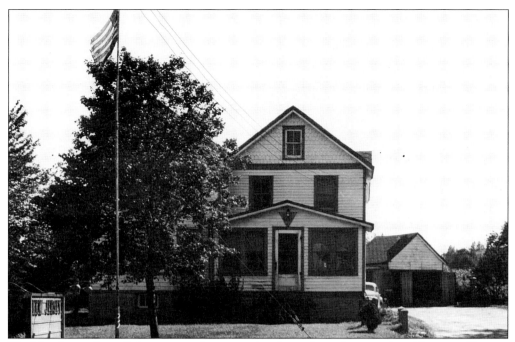

The New Jersey State Police operated a state police barracks in the township. The name Raritan Township was not used due to potential confusion with other Raritans in the state. Since Hazlet was not yet well known, the more recognizable name of "Keyport State Police" was used. Here is the barracks in 1945. The building is still standing today next to the Sea Gull Restaurant. A few years later the police barracks operations were relocated to the former Yate's house on the north side of the highway.

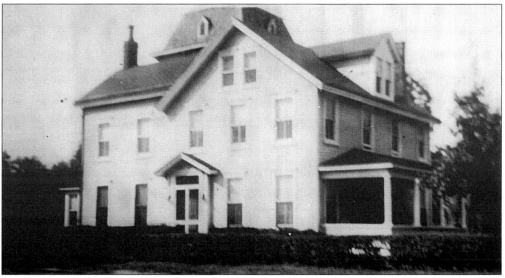

Here is the Keyport State Police Barracks at the former Yate's house. The state police barracks operated at this location until 1971, when operations were relocated to a new building on Highway No. 35 in Holmdel, still under the name of "Keyport." The Keyport State Police unit closed a few years later. The Yate's building was torn down in 1976, and this is now the site of Jiffy Lube.

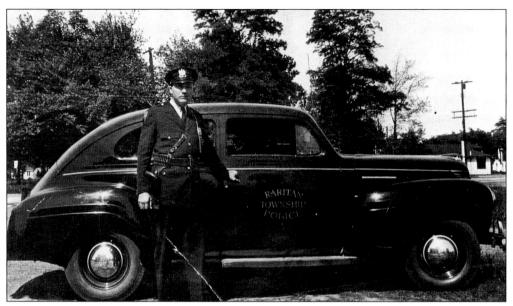

Woodlyne "Woody" Bowne poses next to his Raritan Township patrol car, in West Keansburg, by John Ambrose's Gas Station. From 1946 to 1951 Woody served as the township's police commissioner. He was also a member of the township committee.

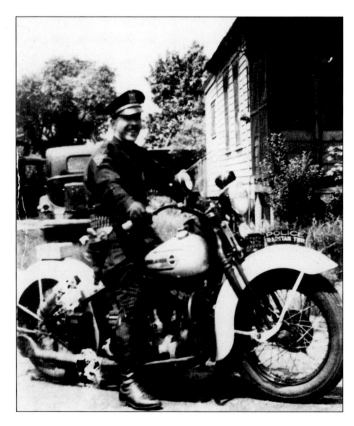

Officer Theodor Franzen is pictured here on his two-year-old 1938 Indian motorcycle.

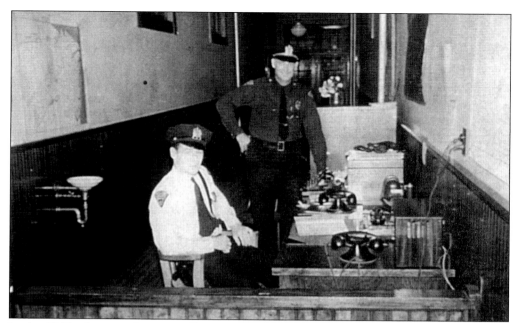

In the 1940s, the township was still too rural to have a full-time police department. Township residents had to rely on the state police. However, the township did have a police department that functioned on weekends during the summer. The township police operated out of the West Keansburg School. In this 1943 photograph at police headquarters inside the school, Captain Stacey Carhart is standing by Patrolman Charles Mack.

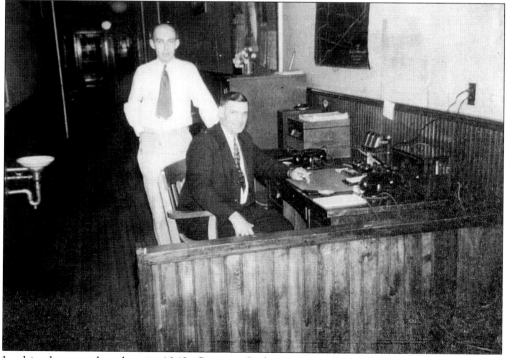

In this photograph, taken in 1942, Captain Carhart is seated with Mayor J. Carlton Cherry standing behind him.

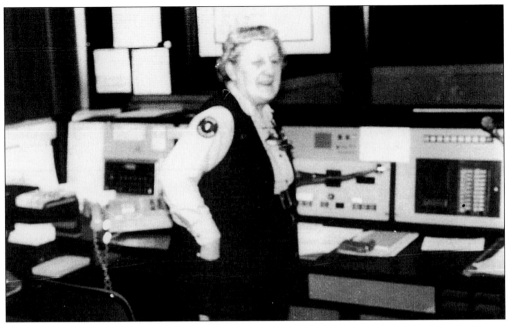

In police headquarters on Middle Road, dispatcher Bertha Cere smiles for the camera.

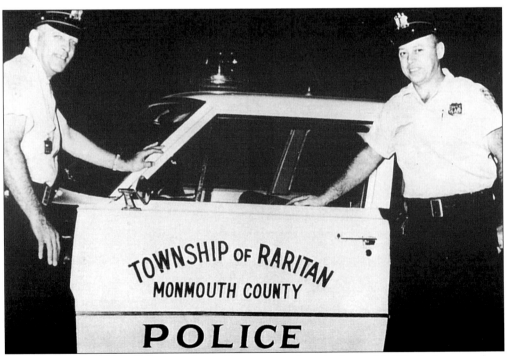

Two patrolmen stand by their township of Raritan patrol car in the mid-1960s. In just two short years, the township police cars would bear the name Hazlet Township.

# *Five*

# Schools and Churches

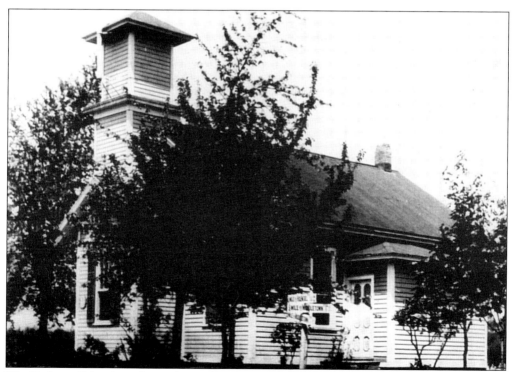

The Bethany School was located near the corner of Bethany Road and Hazlet Avenue. It is one of the oldest buildings still standing (private residence) used as a school.

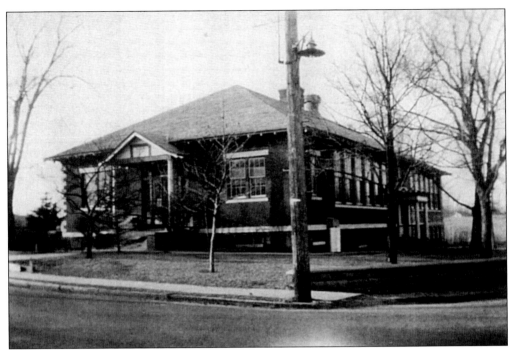

In 1918, the single-room Hazlet School was replaced by this brick building. The new school building initially had two classrooms, but was eventually expanded to four rooms. This photograph was taken after the expansion.

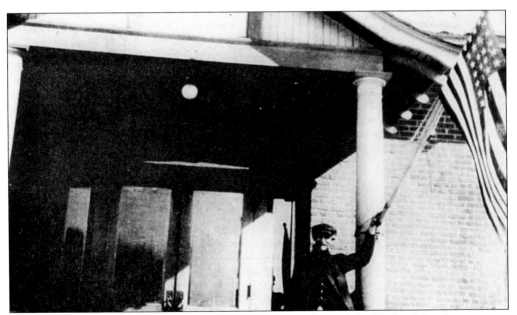

The American flag is shown here proudly being flown in front of the Hazlet School.

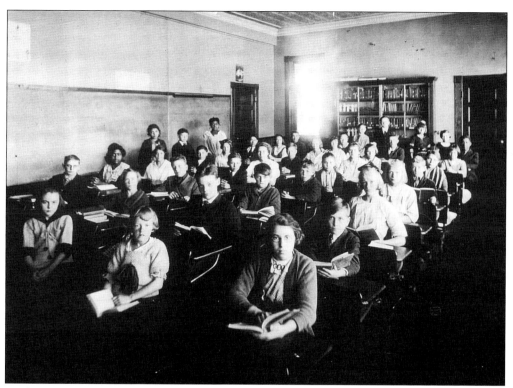

Students posed at their desks for this photograph in 1919, inside a classroom at the Hazlet School.

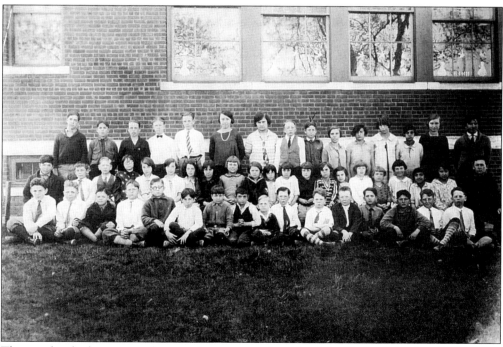

The weather looks warm as these students pose at the side of the Hazlet School in 1933.

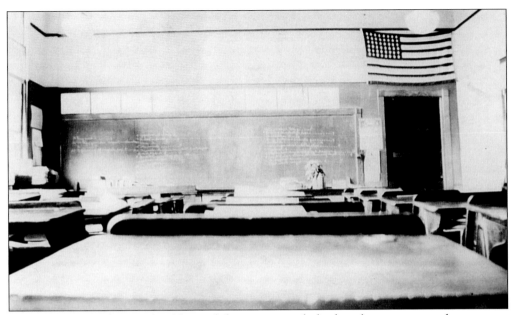

This is a view of what you would see while sitting at a desk, though in an empty classroom, at the Hazlet School.

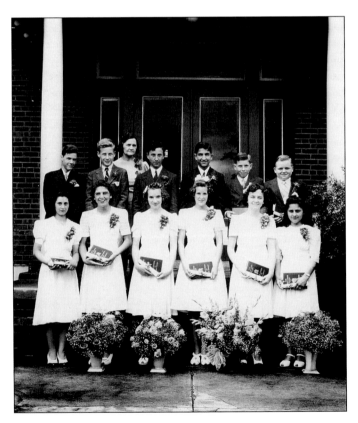

Students pose for graduation in this 1942 photograph. Listed from left to right are as follows: (front row) Ann DeMario, Mary Siano, Ann Dean, Marjorie Smally, Valleria Goetz, and Tina Miele; (back row) Harold Disbrow, George Dunn, Mrs. Bozart (teacher), Sal LaSapio, Jim Straniero, Donald Metzger, and Jack Warnock.

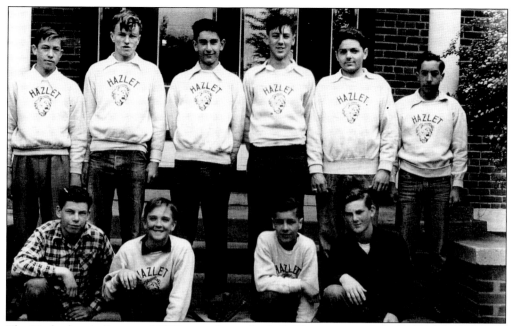

The Hazlet baseball team of 1950 is ready to play ball. They are standing on the front entrance steps of the Hazlet School.

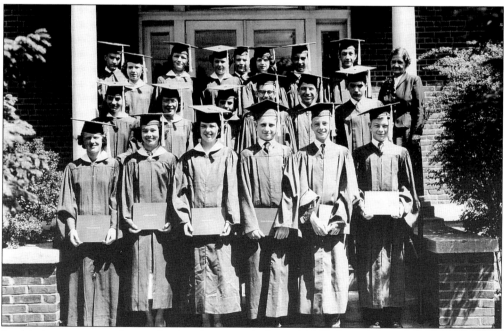

In this image we see the graduating (grammar) class of 1953. Listed from left to right are as follows: (front row) Carole Phillips, Barbara McDonough, Judy Metzger, Roger Stopkie, Alan Bottger, and Donald Ahlers; (middle row) Alice Miro, Sally Webb, Clem Montagna, Bill Meisner, Fred Tortorici, and Vincent Serpico; (back row) Robert Poling, Carol Mowery, Elizabeth Eigenraugh, Julia Kurica, Joe Vogellus, Cecila Mioduszewski, Frank Miele, Julius De Rosa, and teacher Mrs. Bozart.

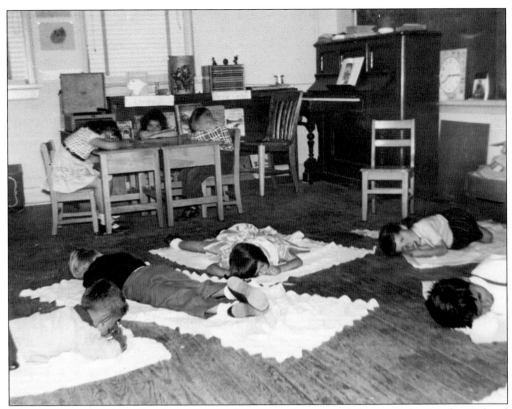

It's nap time for these kindergarten students on the ground floor of the Hazlet School in 1956. This ground-floor (basement) classroom had its own entrance at the rear of the school building.

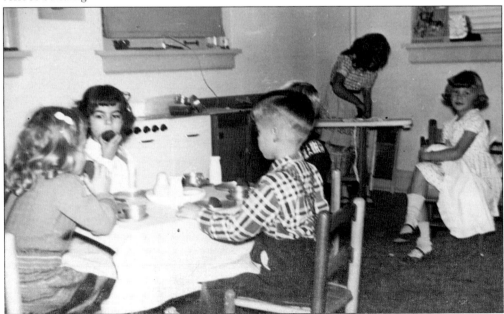

Kindergarten students play kitchen in the Hazlet School.

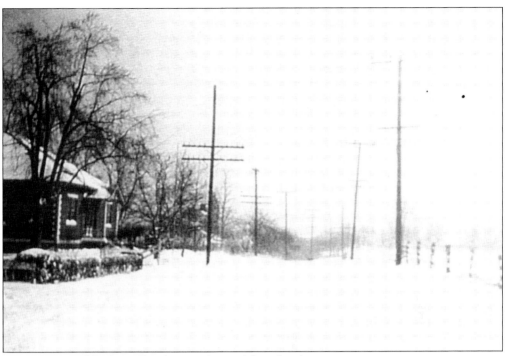

A snow-covered Bethany Road sits in front of the school.

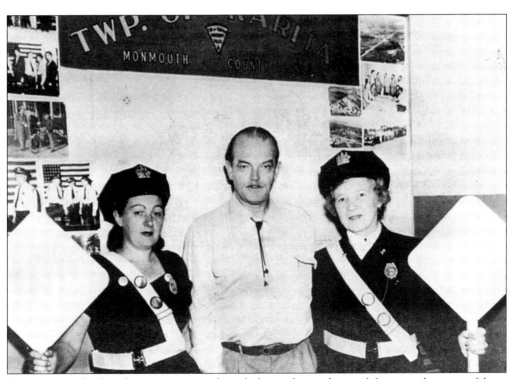

Crossing guards played an important role in helping the students of the township get safely to and from school. Guards pose in uniform holding their stop signs.

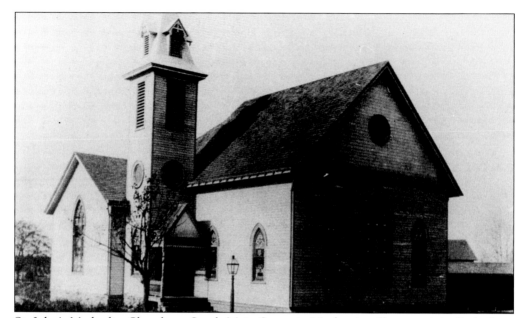

St. John's Methodist Church on South Main Street in Mechanicsville was originally built in 1822 in Holmdel Township, and was called the Bethany Meeting House. It was moved to this location in 1869. The building was destroyed by fire in 1963. A new church was built on the corner of Florence Avenue and South Main Street the following year.

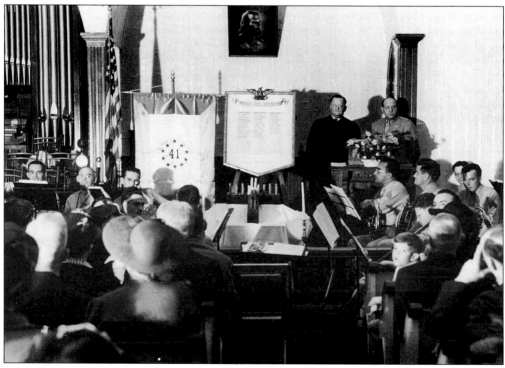

Inside the original St. John's Church servicemen perform music as a plaque for veterans is unveiled.

For many years, the Reverend Norman Riley served as pastor of St. John's Methodist Church.

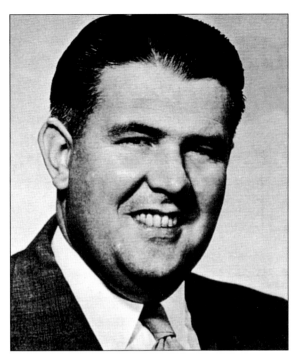

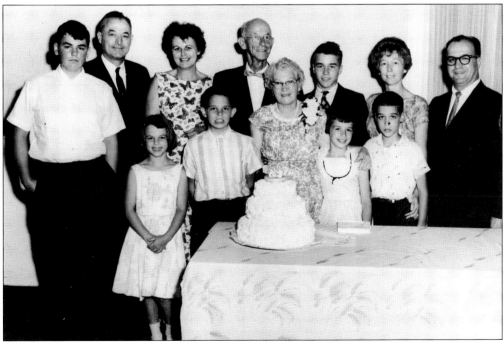

St. John's had a recreation hall that was available for all kinds of functions. Here, Hazlet residents Mr. and Mrs. William Campbell celebrate their 50th wedding anniversary, with their children and grandchildren, in 1961. Listed from left to right are as follows: (front row) Sinclair Campbell, Bill Campbell, Laura Belle Campbell, Kathy Longo, and Bill Longo; (back row) Andy Campbell, Blair Campbell, Madelin Campbell, William Campbell, Doug Longo, Mary Longo (nee Campbell), and Ted Longo.

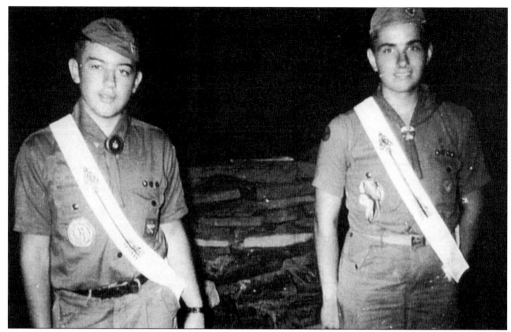

St. John's also had boy scout troop number 135. In this photograph, Al Perdue and Bob Windsor are inducted into the "Order of the Arrow."

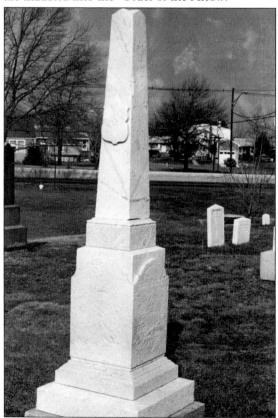

At the Raritan Cemetery, next to the property of St. John's United Methodist Church, is the grave of Dr. John Hazlett (spelled two t's).

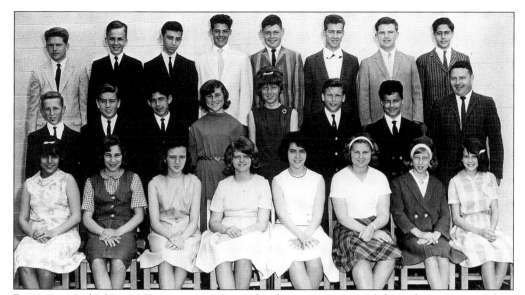

Beginning in the late 1950s, many grammar schools were constructed throughout the township. Here is the Beers Street School's eighth-grade graduating Class of 1964. From left to right they are as follows: (front row) Santina Tortorici, Diane Alfieri, Anna Viscusi, Marlene Carhuff, Nancy Cherry, Angela Miller, Karen Alpaugh, and Linda White; (middle row) Chris Cullen, Bobby Ross, Joe Triguero, Jacueline McNulty, Frances Sherin, Ron Korker, Bobby Page, and teacher Walter Knittel; (back row) Fred Brown, Pete Carnes, Ed Trixeira, Larry Alexander, Scott Roberts, Rony Bertotti, Pete Piatti, and Jerry Johnson.

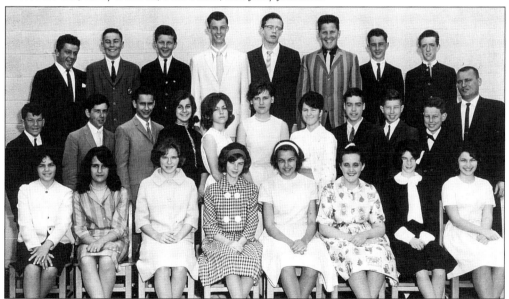

In this photograph are more eighth-grade graduates. From left to right they are as follows: (front row) Diana Ferrante, Louisa Cardone, Maureen Bird, Sharon Horan, Linda Roper, Carmen Morelli, Corinne Noonan, and Agnes Dellapietro; (middle row) Ed Shown, Joe Borges, Lou Costa, Fran Agresta, Denise Tilton, Debbie Jorbel, Colleen Russo, Bill Longo, Jimmy Wales, Drew McCaskey, and teacher Anthony Benetsky; (back row) Bill Denker, Mike Valges, Glen Waltsak, Russ Yess, Joe Dougherty, Ron Kowalski, Tom Loughrey, and John Van Orden.

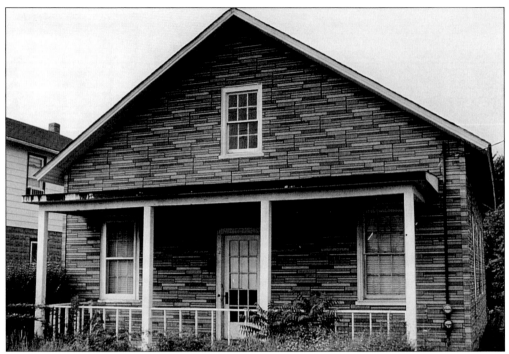

This house on Bethany Road used to be the Bethany School. It was moved from the corner of Bethany Road and Hazlet Avenue to make room for the larger school in 1918, and has been a private residence ever since.

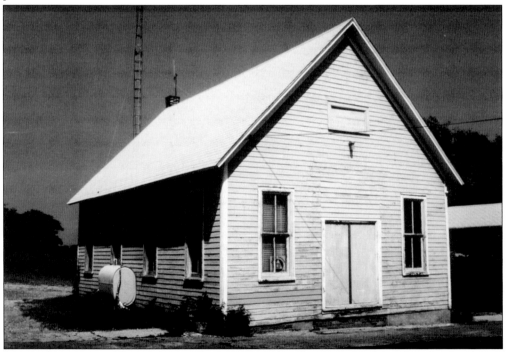

This building on Middle Road, near the Raritan High School, used to be a church. The church closed in 1968, and 10 years later the building was demolished.

# *Six*

# The People

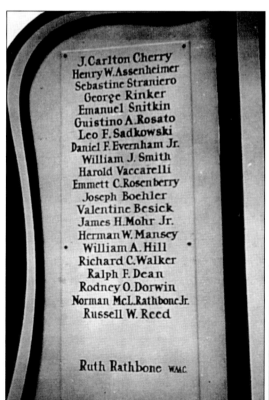
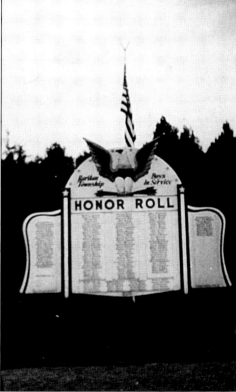

J. Carlton Cherry
Henry W. Assenheimer
Sebastine Straniero
George Rinker
Emanuel Snitkin
Guistino A. Rosato
Leo F. Sadkowski
Daniel F. Evernham Jr.
William J. Smith
Harold Vaccarelli
Emmett C. Rosenberry
Joseph Boehler
Valentine Besick
James H. Mohr Jr.
Herman W. Mansey
William A. Hill
Richard C. Walker
Ralph F. Dean
Rodney O. Dorwin
Norman McL. Rathbone Jr.
Russell W. Reed

Ruth Rathbone wac

This is a plaque at Laurel Avenue and Highway No. 36, proudly displaying the names of the township's veterans who have served their country. A World War II honor roll is to the right.

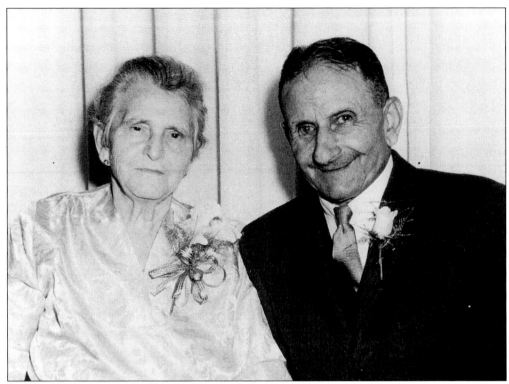

Mr. and Mrs. Mocci pose here for a photograph on November 10, 1962, on the occasion of their 50th wedding anniversary. As indicated earlier, Joe Mocci and his family operated a farm on Bethany Road.

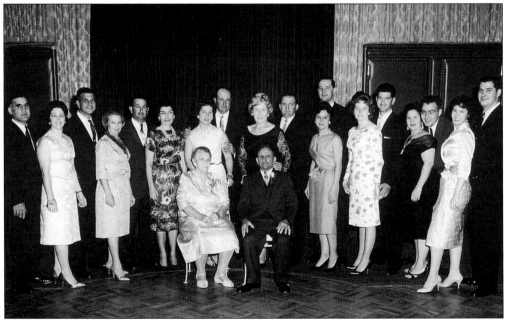

The children, and their spouses, of Mr. and Mrs. Mocci pose for a family photograph at the celebration of their 50th wedding anniversary.

Mr. and Mrs. J. Carlton Cherry are pictured here on their wedding day in 1945. Mr. Cherry served during World War II as an administrative assistant to General Douglas MacArthur in the General Army Headquarters, South Pacific. Locally, Mr. Cherry served as a township committeeman and mayor. In the early 1960s, he was instrumental in getting additional passenger trains to stop in Hazlet, which was warranted after the township's population explosion began. He also helped launch a campaign to change the name of the township to Hazlet Township, which became a reality on November 19, 1967.

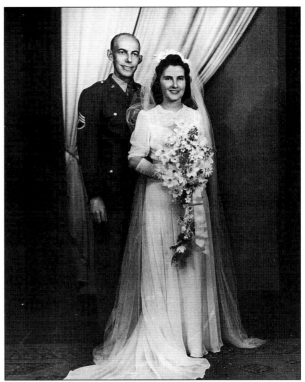

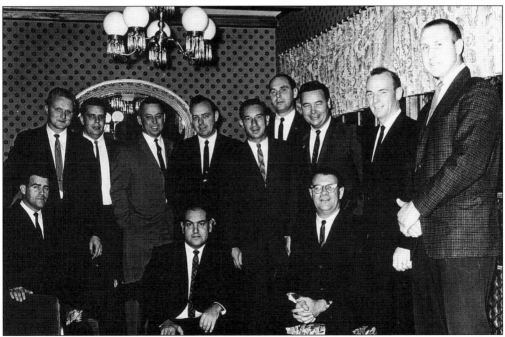

Friends gather at the retirement dinner of special township police officer Joe Kuhl (seated bottom right) in 1963. From left to right are as follows: (front row) Henry Springsteen, Sam Straniero, and Joe Kuhl; (back row) John Nicholl, Don Warren, Vern Manning, Bobby Thorne, Tony D'Ambrosio, Warren Roggerman, Rod Gunther, Bill Smith, and Ed Schramm.

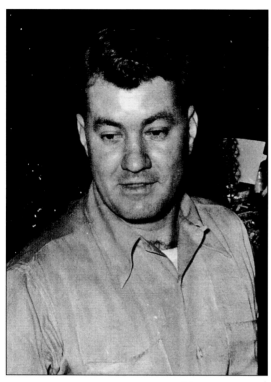

Lawrance J. Nolan (Lawrance with two a's), a local builder, was also the owner and operator of the Lakeview on Highway 36 next to Natco Lake, where the Lakeside Manor stands today.

Mrs. Mary Longo (nee Campbell) is pictured here with her three children in 1958. She was raised in Seattle, WA, where she met her husband, J. Theodore Longo of Matawan, NJ, while he was serving in the U.S. Army. They were married in 1942, just before Mr. Longo left to serve in the South Pacific in World War II. After the war they moved to New Jersey, settling in Hazlet in 1951. Mrs. Longo began teaching for the township in 1956, educating the children of the new population at both the Hazlet School and the Beers Street School. She retired in 1980.

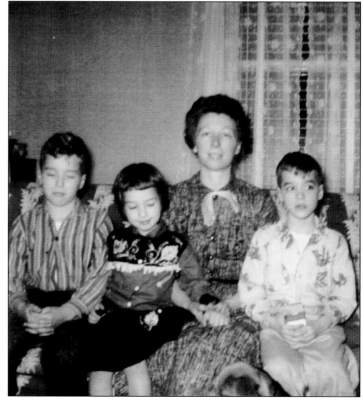

Mr. and Mrs. Fred Dean are photographed here standing in front of their house on Bethany Road. Mr. Dean was operator of Dean's Garage next to their house. He also served at one time as janitor of the Hazlet School.

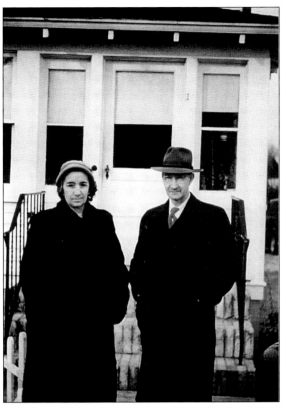

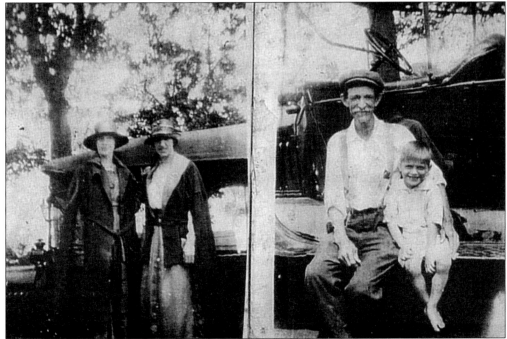

In the left image, two women were photographed posing for a picture on a sunny day. In the right photograph, John Hertle and a young Lloyd Reya Sr. sit on the running board of a car.

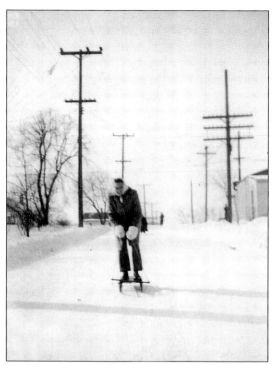

Ann Dean is sliding down a snow-covered Bethany Road in 1940. The building on the right, close to the road, is the grocery store of Frank Hertle, who is Ann Dean's uncle. Snow or no snow, this scene could never take place now as Bethany Road is always crowded with traffic.

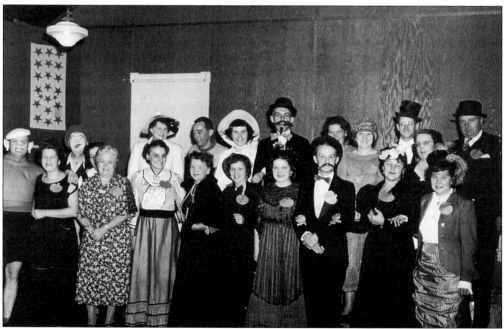

Members of the "Meat and Eat" club met at the Hazlet Firehouse in 1950 for a Halloween party. Listed from left to right they are as follows: (front row) Jim Neidinger, Laneta Neidinger, Edna Peseux, Josie Calt, Mary Calt, Helen Urstadt, Evelyn Ackerson, Rudy Chval, Rose Chval, and Doris Ackerson; (back row) Ernest Peseux, Gen Monahan, Kay Darland, Bud Monahan, Lillian Cherry, J. Carlton Cherry, Dot Bahrenburg, Ethel Smale, Walter Smale, Cele Rothbart, and Ralph Rothbart.

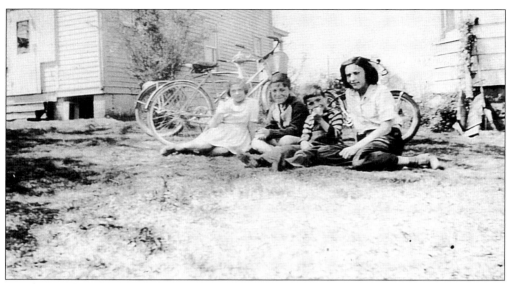

Members of the Miele family—Ann, Larry, Frank, and Marie—pose by their bicycles on a sunny day in 1944.

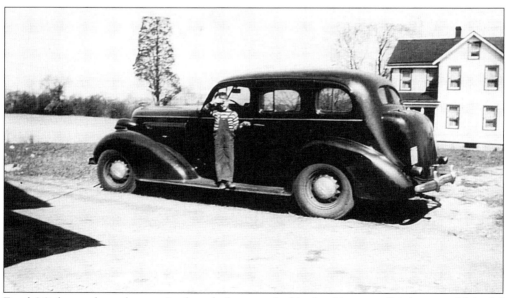

Frank Miele stands on the running board of a car parked in the driveway of his home on Holmdel Road in 1944. The house in the background is the Mione residence.

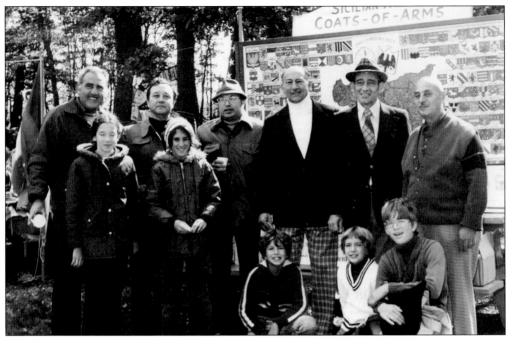

A Columbus Day celebration was photographed at Veterans Park.

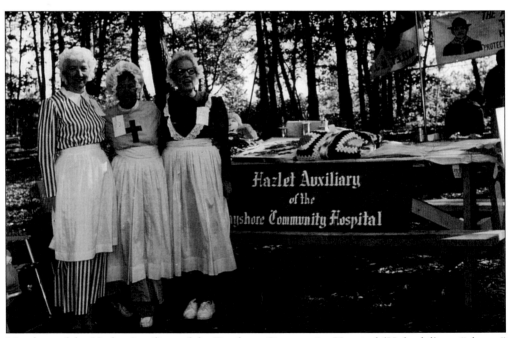

Members of the Hazlet Auxiliary of the Bayshore Community Hospital (Holmdel) say "cheese" while posing for a photograph at Veterans Park. They are Dorothy Scalzo, Lucille Coyle, and Agnes Jannarone.

## Seven

# The Later Years:
# A Community Emerges

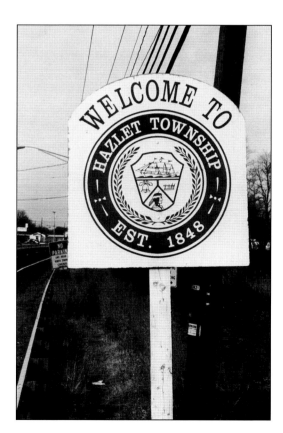

Motorists using Highway No. 36 are welcomed to the township under the name the township has been known as since 1967.

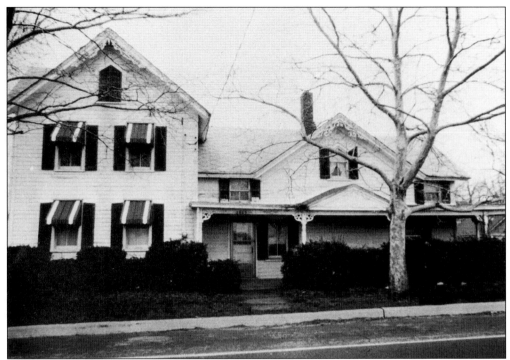

A farmhouse practically sits on Highway 35 near Fleetwood Drive. The township's rural character was diminishing due to suburban sprawl and, as can be seen here, the recently widened highway was creeping up this farmer's property.

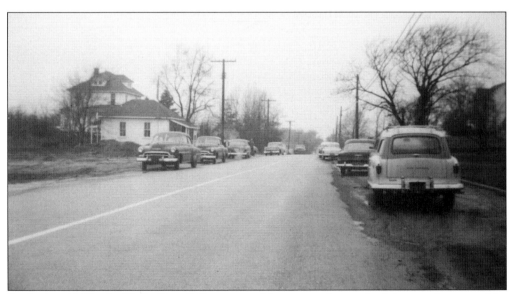

By the late 1950s, the Hazlet Post Office was unable to meet the needs of the growing township, as evidenced by the number of cars parked by post office patrons on Holmdel Road. City-type mail deliveries for Hazlet were established in 1959, the same year post office operations were moved to temporary quarters at the Hazlet Firehouse. A new permanent post office was constructed on Hazlet Avenue in 1961.

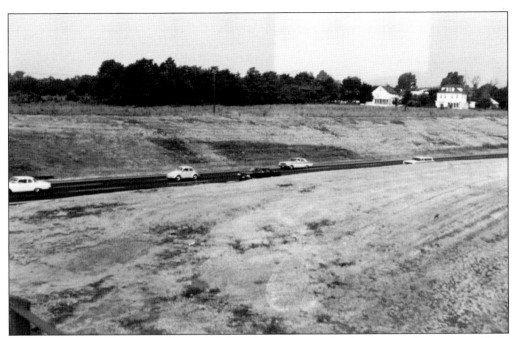

The biggest event to impact the township and hurl it toward suburbia was the opening of the Garden State Parkway in 1954. For residents of the township, an automobile trip to northern New Jersey or New York City would no longer mean crawling on congested highways. The new superhighway cut such trips significantly, and caused the township's open farmland to become prime real estate for massive housing developments. In this photograph, northbound cars leave Hazlet.

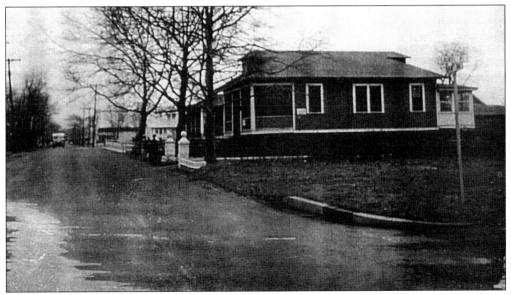

Laurel Avenue in the 1960s was quite different from the dirt roadway of the 1930s. The house on the right in the distance is from a housing development which had been built shortly before this photograph was taken.

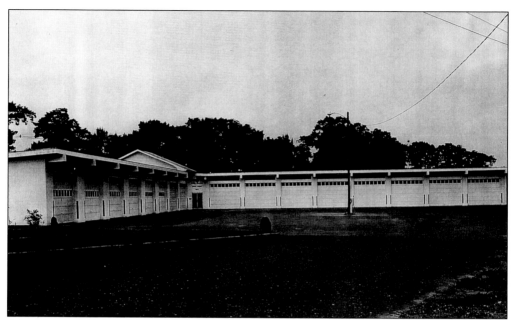

After the township had grown, residents needed the service of a full-time department of public works. Here is a view of the 16-bay public works building on Leocadia Court in 1973.

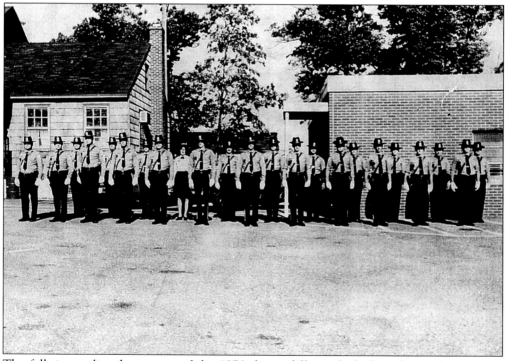

The full-time police department of the 1970s has a different look from the weekend police department of 20 years earlier. Members of the Hazlet Police Department pose for a group shot at the township hall/police station on Middle Road.

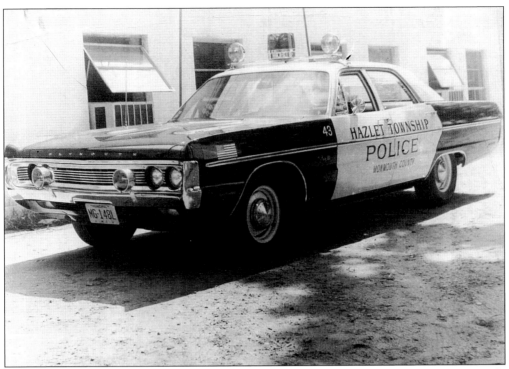

Hazlet Township police car number 43 sits behind the police station on Middle Road, ready for action.

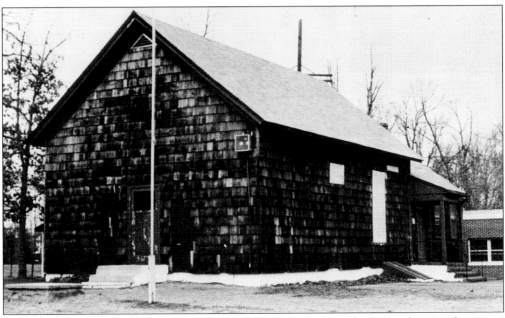

Here is the public library of the township in 1970. If the building looks familiar, it is because a photograph of this building appeared earlier as the township hall and former North Centerville School. Today the building is gone, as the township library moved to a new building a quarter of a mile west on Middle Road.

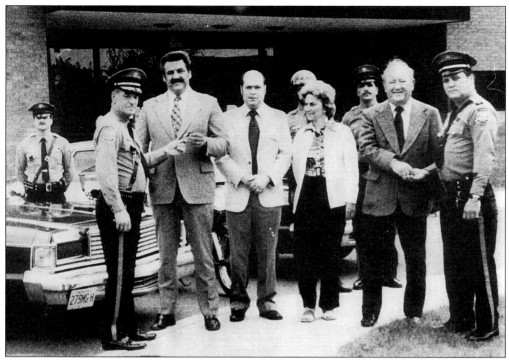

Police and township officials gather in front of the new police station and municipal court building, which opened in 1975.

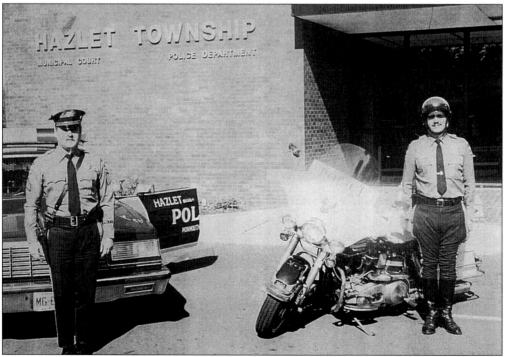

Two policemen with a police car and a motorcycle also pose in front of the new police headquarters and municipal court building.

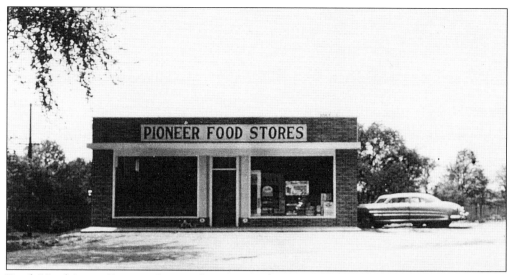

Frank Hertle's new Pioneer Grocery Store is seen here after the business moved across Holmdel Road into a larger building. Frank Hertle's son, Frank Jr., continued the business after his father died in 1972. He sold the store in 1980. The building is now the home of Brother's Deli.

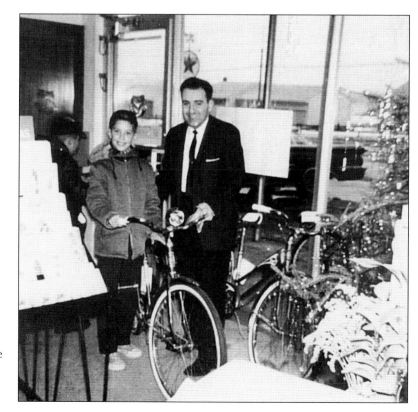

Tony Jackapino, pharmacist and owner of Hazlet Pharmacy, congratulates 9-year-old John Aque inside the pharmacy. John had won a bicycle in a drawing sponsored by the pharmacy.

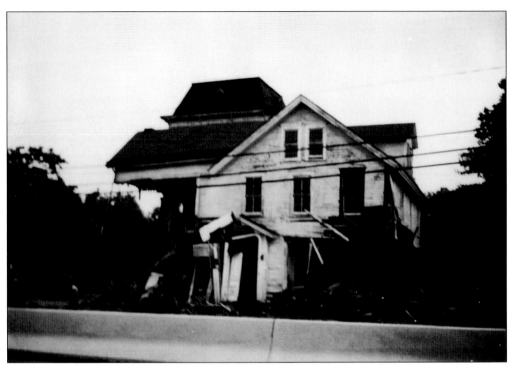

The old Yate's house and former Keyport State Police Barracks, on Highway No. 35, is pictured here as it was being torn down in 1976. Today Jiffy Lube is at this location.

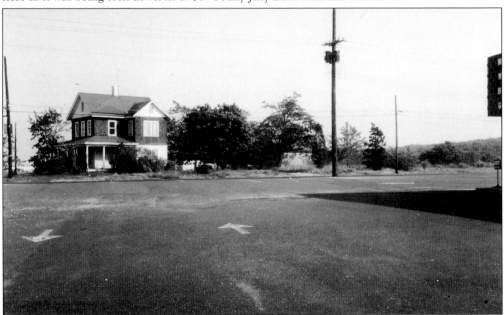

An all-too-familiar sight in the township since the 1950s—an old farmhouse boarded up and ready to be demolished to make room for a mall or a highway-widening project. In the foreground, where a garden of fresh vegetables once stood, is a paved parking lot for a shoe store. This is now the site of Pier 1 Imports and Hollywood Video, at the corner of Highway No. 35 and Bethany Road.

From 1952 to 1979, this structure served as the township's passenger railroad depot. The "waiting room" may have been air-conditioned in the winter and heated in the summer, but the shelter did protect railroad patrons from the rain.

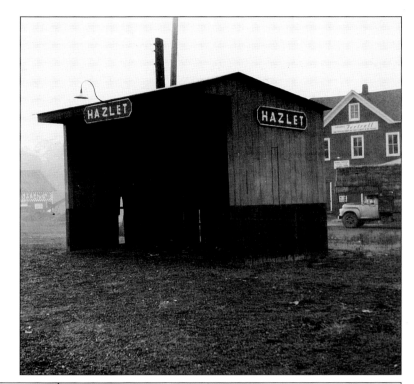

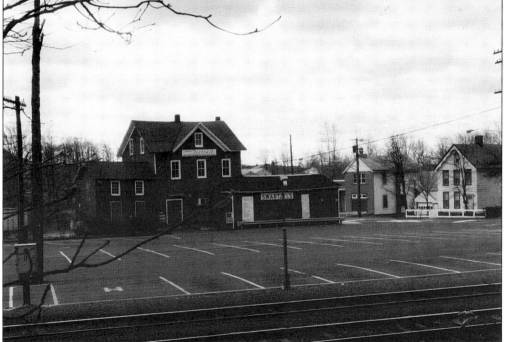

Here in 1970, the township paved the dirt, gravel, dusty, and sometimes muddy rail commuter parking lot. In 1960, only a few dozen commuters boarded trains at Hazlet, but by 1970 the number had grown to several hundred. Commuters were provided new parking facilities, which also included improved lighting.

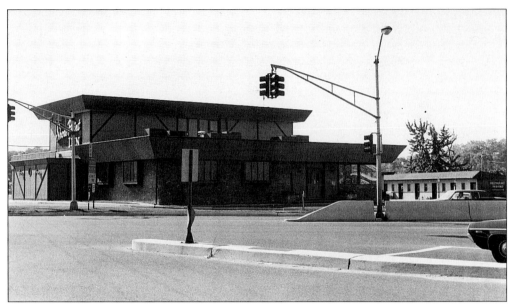

This is the new Shore Point Inn around 1973. The structure was built to replace the older structure, which was destroyed by fire in 1965. This is the site of the former Old Dutch Tavern. As indicated earlier, this was The Cove II from 1995 to 1997, and is now the Sea Gull.

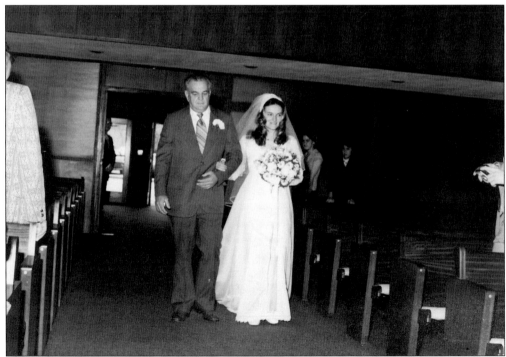

Lona Joyce and her dad, Forrest Hornsby, walk down St. John's United Methodist Church aisle on April 16, 1977, 13 years after the first wedding took place in the new building.

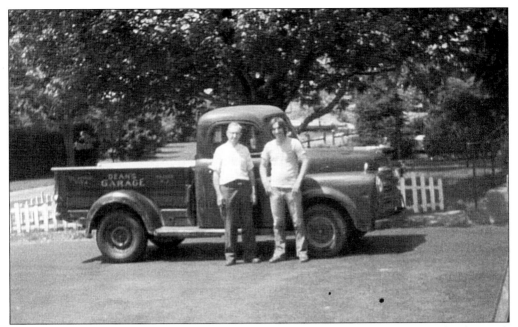

Roger Mills (right) is pictured here with his grandfather, Fred Dean. Roger bought the truck from his grandfather, then drove it to Savannah.

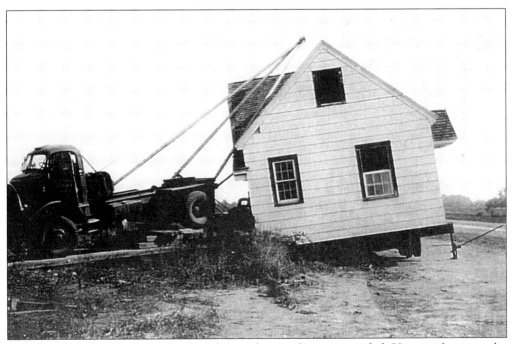

More businesses sprang up in the township as the population expanded. Here is a house in the process of being moved from Tinton Falls to its eventual final destiny on Laurel Avenue and Bauer Street. It would become a beauty parlor.

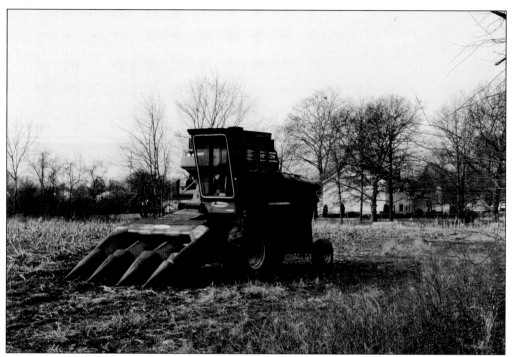

The township has still retained some farms. Here a modern plow sits at a corn farm in a field off Stone Road.

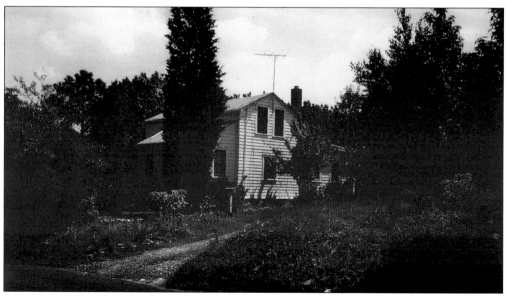

One of the oldest houses in the township is located on Clark Street near the Garden State Parkway entrance. It is shown here in 1975.

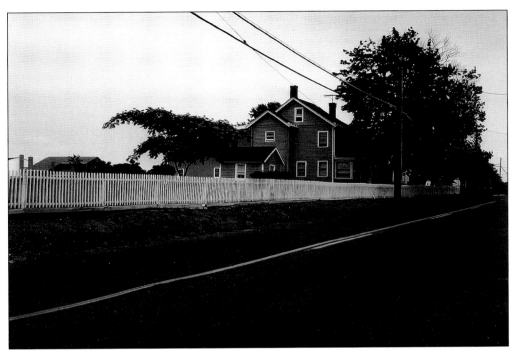

An old farmhouse on Beers Street, in 1978, is nestled next to a housing development built just a year earlier. The roofs of the houses can be seen to the left just above the tops of the picket fence. A blend of the township's rural past and its bedroom community is present.

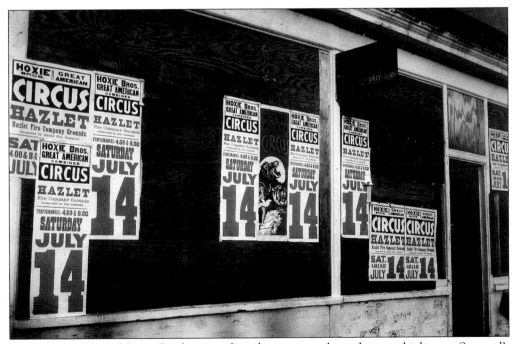

With strip malls and larger hardware and garden centers along the area highways, Swartzel's Hardware and Garden Supply Store closed in the late 1970s. Here, in July of 1984, the boarded up windows are plastered with posters advertising a circus that has come to town!

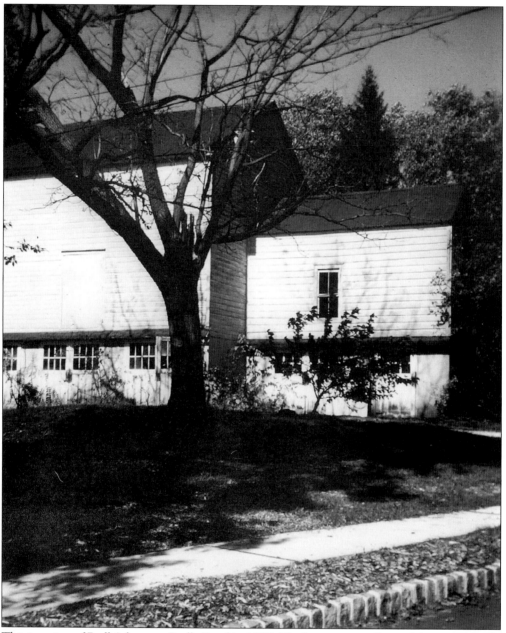

This is a view of Bedle's barn on Bedle Road in 1978. The barn is typically rural, however, Bedle Road has the look of a suburban roadway, with its curbing and sidewalks. This is yet another instance of side-by-side examples of the past and present captured on film.